The Only Airbnb Investing Guide You Will Need

Learn How to Start, Manage, and Fully Automate a Profitable Airbnb Business to Quit Your Job and Stop Trading Your Time for Money Even With No Experience

Richard Hedberg

Table of Contents

Your Free Gift

As a way of saying thanks for your purchase, I'm offering the eBook, *Strategies to Grow Your Airbnb Business Fast*, for FREE to my readers.

To get instant access, just go to:
https://prosperwithrichard.com/Airbnb-free-bonus

Inside this eBook you will discover:

- A list of Airbnb business tools that will save you hours on preparing your Airbnb listing and living space.
- The secret Airbnb investing strategies that the experts swear by.
- Advice on how to navigate through any complaints that come your way.
- Helpful checklists that will keep you organized.
- And so much more!

If you want to increase your Airbnb income, make sure to grab your free eBook.

Introduction

In today's economy, millions of people work at jobs they don't enjoy but need to survive. To avoid getting stuck in a monotonous job and depending solely on a paycheck, people need to think outside the box. Financial independence can change people's lives and help them pursue what they truly love.

Are you someone who doesn't just want to rely on a day job to support your family, personal expenses, and savings? Are you someone who is willing to work hard and do your best to achieve financial independence? Are you someone who wants to help people find a great place to stay when they need it? Then you have come to the right place. I will be teaching you about Airbnb and how it has broadened the possibilities of the hospitality industry, and how it has the potential to change your life, too.

Airbnb is an online service that links people to host properties where they stay as guests. With millions of new listings every year, Airbnb entrepreneurs are making hundreds of thousands of dollars in profits utilizing vision and commitment. In addition to providing an opportunity, Airbnb also provides a means for you to achieve your personal goals. This is because you will no longer have to work a day job to make ends meet. You can quit your dead-end job and pursue your real passions instead.

In spite of the fact that the Airbnb business looks basic from afar, once you start to host your own properties and wait for guests, you will realize there are several things you need to know to succeed. Not everyone has a successful mentor as a friend or a family member. You need someone who will provide you with information about what to do and what not to do to become a successful Airbnb entrepreneur… and that's me!

I am Richard Hedberg, and I am happy to say that I am a veteran host in the Airbnb business. I have hosted more than five properties and have helped hundreds of guests have a once-in-a-lifetime experience during their stays. With more than six years of experience in the short-term rental business, I have gained enough practical knowledge about the Airbnb business to write a book about it. I wanted to help people who are struggling to earn their first pennies in this Airbnb industry.

If you're reading this book, you are probably trying to figure out whether you're right for this business. Most people are curious about themselves, and personal reflection is always necessary when considering career goals.

This book will help you become a pro in the Airbnb hosting business if you are:

- passionate about learning the basics and implementing them practically

- interested in learning how every detail in your business affects your bookings
- interested in learning the fundamentals of Airbnb's short-term rental business
- a person who loves research and wants to ensure their business will beat their competitors and move up in the rankings fast
- a person who strives to succeed and works hard
- a person who wants to break free from dependency on paychecks and move toward financial independence

If you are in one or all of these categories, then I am happy to tell you that this book will help you understand the nuances of the Airbnb business. It will push you to become the best host in your area and earn profits in less time. This book has all the important information you must learn to become a successful host in terms of both financial returns and personal satisfaction. Becoming an Airbnb host with consistent bookings will not be easy. However, with the strategies provided in this book, you will be able to dominate your competitors and enter the top 1% of current hosts.

This book will cover the following important lessons:

- what it takes to get started in the Airbnb business
- finding properties that will fit your needs and goals
- understanding what you are getting into from the get-go
- planning everything out for your rental business
- gaining the tools you will need to be successful in the Airbnb business

- learning about marketing and networking techniques that will help you to not only attract guests but also build your reputation
- thinking outside the box and scaling your business
- automating your business so that you won't have to do all the hard work
- learning shortcuts to make your hosting experience better with the help of a project management company
- understanding the nitty-gritty, such as taxes and insurance
- getting a complete look at all the necessary aspects like cleaning, amenities, and regulations
- step-by-step instructions to create a listing and craft the perfect headline and description
- learning to choose photos that will give you a competitive advantage over other listings
- …and a lot of other interesting topics that will help both new and experienced hosts—beginners will gain the confidence to start, and experienced hosts will learn how to take their business to the next level

To help you even more, we will also provide a list of important Airbnb tools, which are available at the end of the book.

How Do I Get the Most Out of this Book?

To get the most from this book, you will need to apply the strategies I've provided to your own listing on Airbnb. A lot of constant verification and checking back needs to happen so you can identify the strategy that is working for you. Just like any business, starting with Airbnb will require some initial capital and a little patience to see real success in the long run.

Before proceeding further, let me provide you with a quick questionnaire that you can use to learn about yourself or use as motivation before reading about the short-term rental business with Airbnb, which is the leader in the market. While this book is written exclusively for those interested in working through Airbnb, you can also use the strategies provided on any other platform, such as VRBO.

Initial Questionnaire:

- Are you passionate about short-term rental properties?
- What is your initial budget for your business?
- Are you willing to do all the work by yourself, or are you interested in outsourcing work to professionals?
- How much are you hoping to earn or save from your Airbnb business income?
- As an Airbnb business owner, what do you hope to accomplish?
- Can you do additional research before starting your Airbnb business?
- Are you willing to spend money on online tools for better research?
- Are you looking forward to interviewing people before hiring them for the jobs you provide?
- Are you tech savvy, and do you understand the different features that the Airbnb website and app offer?

Chapter 1

An Overview of Airbnb Investing

In the early 2000s, three guys in San Francisco started a small business by renting out their living room to guests who slept on their air mattresses. By hosting their friends and guests in a saturated market at competitive prices, they quickly won more customers than they had anticipated. This idea was further developed and soon turned into a startup entity named Airbnb. Brian Chesky, Joe Gebbia, and Nathan Blecharczyk are the founders of Airbnb, which is now the most popular home-sharing platform in the world. What was once a startup now offers more listings than all the premium hotel brands around the world combined.

When Brian Chesky, Joe Gebbia, and Nathan Blecharczyk started to rent out their living room, they had no idea what kind of wave they would create in the tourism and hospitality industry. Fast forward 15 years, and it has convinced hundreds of thousands of people around the world to list their homes and properties so that tourists and enthusiasts can experience a personal stay with more freedom and fewer restrictions.

What is Airbnb, and How Does it Work?

Airbnb is a web and mobile platform that works with the primary goal of connecting people who are looking to stay in a home or property with someone who is renting their properties. It was created through the inspiration of a special kind of economic system known as the "sharing economy."

In a sharing economy, a service is provided by one individual and another individual utilizes those services. To ensure that everything goes smoothly in terms of transactions and safety, a centralized peer usually exists. Airbnb is an example of a centralized peer that monitors both hosts and guests so that the process flows as smoothly as possible. In exchange for their services, these centralized peers charge a fee to both hosts and guests in this example.

Innovations like Airbnb work in a consumer-to-consumer business model instead of the business-to-consumer model that is used by traditional companies. While the sharing economy was popularized by Uber, Airbnb has also seen tremendous success, especially in the U.S.

Services like Airbnb focus mainly on providing a platform to help both individuals on either side of a transaction to meet in the marketplace.

What are Short-Term Rentals?

The Airbnb service connects guests with hosts who want to rent their property on a short-term basis.

For your property to qualify for Airbnb hosting, it will need to meet the following requirements that are closely related to the model of short-term rentals.

- **Furnished**

The space that you are renting needs to be furnished with the basic essential amenities. Guests need to be comfortable during their stay and feel satisfied with the furniture and appliances you have provided.

- **Transient Occupancy**

From a technical point of view, your property can be considered for a short-term rental service as long as the guests book the property for less than 30 days. If the guest books your property for more than 30 days and up to six months, then the booking will be considered a mid-term rental. Airbnb allows mid-term rentals for certain listings. A long-term booking is one that lasts more than six months, and this is not that common with Airbnb.

What Do I Need to Host on Airbnb?

To host on Airbnb, you need to first satisfy the conditions listed below. If you are missing any of these, it will be difficult for you to break even in the Airbnb business.

- **A Space**

The most important criterion for hosting on Airbnb is that you need a space or a property for guests to stay in. Even outdoor spaces can be hosted for guests who are on a tight budget. However, to earn consistent bookings and good profits, you need to have a good property that is well furnished.

- **A Listing**

Before you can invite guests to your property, you need to first create a listing on the Airbnb platform. Once the listing goes live, guests can book your property for their preferred available dates so that they can stay according to their plans.

- **Right Tools**

For your Airbnb business to become a success, you need to use certain tools that we have provided throughout this book. Tools can help you automate your business workflow and make the process much more efficient and organized for you.

- **Right Strategies**

Your business profit potential will completely depend on the strategies that you use to manage your Airbnb business. This book helps you to understand different strategies that can assist you in successfully managing your hosting business with Airbnb.

Why Should I Consider Airbnb?

While there are several other short-term rental services, such as booking.com, Airbnb has been the most successful in the industry due to the reasons mentioned below. Knowing them can help you understand why Airbnb is usually the best choice for hosting guests in your properties.

- Airbnb as a brand is more popular than any other service, making it nearly a household name.
- Airbnb provides insurance protection for up to $1 million, making it tough to recommend other services.

- The Airbnb platform is easy to use, as its UI is minimal and designed to be used by users of any age. It has both mobile and web apps, so more users depend on it to find properties for their stay.
- Airbnb provides an additional communication layer to mediate any disputes that may arise between the guests and the hosts.
- Airbnb also charges fewer service fees when compared to other services, making it hard to recommend anyone else.
- Airbnb doesn't restrict the listings based on the property type. From villas to outdoor spaces, anything can be hosted on Airbnb.
- The community on Airbnb is friendly, as most of the hosts are willing to help beginners. You can easily network with other Airbnb hosts in your area to improve your bookings and learn from others.

Is Airbnb Safe for Hosts?

You may have some doubts as a first-time host about whether or not it is safe to allow strangers into your property. There will always be nightmare guests, but with the $1 million protection Airbnb provides, rest assured that most often, nothing bad is going to happen, and if your property is damaged, you will be covered for the loss under Airbnb's conditions. This $1 million Airbnb protection is available in all countries where it operates.

Airbnb also has developed safety features to help hosts feel more confident and less worried. Let's take a look at some of them.

- **There is no exchange of cash.**

All the transactions will be handled directly on the Airbnb platform when guests book a listing. As Airbnb acts as an intermediary, it is impossible for guests to scam you by staying and not paying for it.

- **Hosts can see the government IDs of the guests.**

Airbnb makes it possible to display the government IDs of the guests you have agreed to host. Airbnb also provides other information such as email and mobile numbers so you can reach out to them independently. If the guests haven't provided these details, you can ask them via messaging on the platform, and if you are not sure about their authenticity, then you can also cancel the booking without any penalty from Airbnb.

- **Hosts have maximum control over requirements.**

When you publish a listing, you get maximum control of how to set your requirements. For example, you can set your own pricing and stay requirements so that you will be able to receive the guests of your preference into your property.

- **Hosts can set their own rules.**

Airbnb doesn't have any mandatory rules that need to be imposed on guests by the hosts. You are free to set any rules according to your liking, providing peace of mind for hosts. You can also set your own security deposit limit so that there is a financial stake that encourages guests to behave properly when they are on your property.

How Can I Make Money on Airbnb?

The business model of Airbnb is quite simple to understand. When you host property on Airbnb for guests, you need to follow the step-by-step procedure given below.

1. Lease a property if you don't already have one.

To host on Airbnb, you need to have access to a property that is complete and that supports the local regulations for short-term rentals.

2. Create a listing.

Once you decide on the property, create a listing with a great headline, cover photo, and complete description of the amenities you provide. When creating a listing, you also need to upload the house rules, pricing, and a guide for the guests.

3. Wait for the bookings.

Once the listing goes live, whenever a potential guest searches for nearby properties in a locality, your listing will show up. With more bookings and positive reviews, your rank on the Airbnb website will increase. Once a guest chooses your listing, Airbnb will automatically notify you.

4. Review the guest details and accept.

Once guests send you a request to book your property, you can quickly go through their profile, as Airbnb also lets hosts review guests, making it easy to avoid any tough guests. Once you have reviewed, you can accept the request and the guest will now be asked to pay the booking price so that the property can be reserved.

5. Make the property ready.

Before the check-in time, hosts usually need to look over their place and ensure that the listing looks perfect for the guests. If you want to make this step easier on yourself, then you can use professional cleaners to do this work for you.

6. Check-in process.

Guests can check in using the pin that is generated by your smart lock. If you don't have a smart lock, then you can just provide them with a key. Once the check-in is completed, you need to answer any questions that guests may ask using the Airbnb message service.

7. Check-out process.

Once the guest is ready to leave, you might give them a small parting gift and complete the check-out process. Once the guests leave, if you find any items missing or broken, then you can open a claim with Airbnb customer service to deduct the amount from the security deposit. If the security deposit is not enough to cover the loss, then the $1 million Airbnb insurance protection can come in handy.

8. Write and receive reviews.

Once the check-out process is completed, the review windows will open for both hosts and guests to review each other. Guests can review your listing and will often include both the positives and negatives according to their experience within 14 days of their check-out. Similarly, you can review the guest based on whether or not they have followed the rules of your property within 14 days of their check-out.

9. Money is released.

Once the guest checks out, the money you have earned will be directly deposited into your Airbnb account and it can then be transferred to your bank account. Airbnb may charge certain taxes according to your country's regulations.

10. Reinvest and scale.

Once you receive a few bookings, you can further invest your profits to lease more listings and scale your business. The potential to make money with Airbnb is infinite if you can automate the process with the help of professional helpers and tools.

How Can Being an Airbnb Host Change My Life?

Being an Airbnb host can be a life-changing experience. There are two main benefits that come from being a host which are mentioned all the time by experienced hosts who have fallen in love with their business.

- **Generate additional income.**

The main reason why many property owners host on Airbnb is to earn some additional income. Irrespective of whether you are hosting on your own property or leasing, it doesn't matter because ultimately your main goal is to earn income from the properties.

- **Meet people from around the world.**

With Airbnb, it becomes possible to meet people from different countries and cultures. You can understand their perspectives and learn interesting things from them, especially if you are hosting them for more than a few weeks. It is possible to network and build lifelong relationships with the guests you have hosted. Lots of hosts have made friends, fallen in love, and even gotten married because of Airbnb hosting! While it is not mandatory to spend time with your guests, it is always an option if they want to socialize and establish a good relationship with you. Depending on the guest's comfort level, you also need to leave them alone if they prefer privacy.

Who is Not Suitable to Host on Airbnb?

While up till now, we have explained why Airbnb can be a good alternative option for you to earn additional income, it is also important for us to explain when it may not suit you.

The following are some factors that may make it hard for you to sustain yourself in the Airbnb business.

- **Your property is not clean or looks very old.**

It is very hard for guests to have a wonderful experience if the property has not been cleaned properly or looks very old because of old, cracked paint. If you are someone who is not willing to hire a professional cleaner or clean the property yourself, then Airbnb hosting is not a good idea for you. Instead, rent your property to someone who wants to live there for a longer period.

- **You don't want to help the guests because you are often busy.**

If you are busy and not interested in communicating with your guests, including answering their queries whenever required, then Airbnb hosting is not a good business opportunity for you. You need to at least hire a virtual assistant to provide the best experience for your guests at all times.

- **You can't handle noise.**

When you allow guests into your property, then it is possible that they will make some noise. This is common when sharing space with your guests, and while you can definitely warn them to not exceed the maximum noise levels, it can be demotivating for some hosts. In addition, if you host friends or relatives often in the same space, then hosting on Airbnb may not be a good idea for you.

- **You are anxious in uncertain situations.**

Running an Airbnb business can sometimes be unpredictable, even if you have made the effort to streamline the business with automation and hired a cleaning service. For example, your property owner might call you suddenly and ask you to shut down the Airbnb listing due to their own reasons. If you are not willing to tackle these uncertain situations, then an Airbnb business might be tough for you to handle.

Different Types of Airbnb Properties and Spaces

Airbnb is constantly evolving, and it has now expanded into three additional categories called Plus, Airbnb Luxe, and Airbnb for Work. While they are similar, they cater to different audiences and require different amenities. If you are interested in leasing a property but are unsure of what type to look for, then read on to learn about the pros and cons for each type of property that can be hosted on Airbnb. Be sure to do some initial research and determine which properties work better in your locality before leasing and listing on Airbnb.

Airbnb Classic

This is the most popular way to host using Airbnb. This book mostly focuses on these properties, as most of the hosts who own or lease properties make them available for guests using this option. Using Airbnb classic, you can rent out one room, a whole floor as a studio apartment, or offer the whole property.

Here are the two most popular options that hosts provide for guests:

- **Entire Place**: When you want to provide the whole property or a villa for your guests so that they have the utmost privacy, then it is listed as an "Entire Place" property on Airbnb. When you offer this, it is a good idea to provide exclusive features for guests, such as better furnishings or a complimentary breakfast.
- **Private Room**: When you have only one room on your property to offer, then you can use this option.

It is one of the cheapest options available for guests on the Airbnb service.

A Unique Stay

When hosts use this option, it means that their property is unique for their specific location. For example, a cottage on a tea plantation is unique and might see higher demand, and therefore it might cost more than the regular properties in the suburban area.

Airbnb for Work

Airbnb recently launched this category for providing rentals in an office or workspace designed for professionals. To become eligible to provide properties for professional work, you need to offer special amenities such as gigabyte Wi-Fi and a dedicated workstation.

Airbnb Plus

Airbnb Plus is the luxurious tier service that Airbnb offers for guests. To list your property in this category, you will have to first pass the quality checks that are performed by the Airbnb team.

Some quality check requirements that Airbnb uses include:

- outstanding amenities
- minimum of 4.8 rating from guests
- booking requests from guests accepted in more than 95% of cases
- supports easy check-in
- no record of canceling confirmed bookings

Airbnb Luxe

Airbnb Luxe is the highest tier that Airbnb offers for its guests There are less than 2,000 properties that have currently been accepted into this category. Airbnb ensures that these listings are of the highest quality by monitoring them with a team using 300 different criteria. While it may be difficult for a beginner to be a part of this program, your ultimate goal with an Airbnb business should be to own one of these properties to welcome guests, as the profit margins are usually very high.

Gaining "Superhost" Status

"Superhosts" are hosts who have a good track record with Airbnb. When guests see this tag, they know they can expect a stay experience that goes above and beyond the norm. You cannot set yourself as a superhost on your profile yourself.

Once you receive adequate bookings, and if most of them are positive, then the Airbnb algorithms will automatically change your status from a host to a "Superhost." While the exact metrics are unavailable, typically, hosts with a 90% response rate and more than 80% five-star reviews are given the superhost position. Becoming a superhost can also help you increase nightly rates without losing bookings.

With a good introduction to Airbnb and the business model out of the way, let's get into learning about the planning stage. All potential Airbnb hosts should follow this advice in order to kickstart their host business. If you've been around for a while, you'll be surprised at how much more you could be doing to increase your bookings and profits.

Chapter 2

The Planning Phase

Airbnb hosts need a well-planned strategy before they dive into the hosting business and welcome guests into their property. Planning will help you understand the positives, negatives, and what you can do to get the most out of your business. This chapter focuses on the fundamental information and tactics related to research, business structures, taxes, insurance, and regulations that you can use to get started the right way as a host in the short-term rental business on Airbnb.

Choosing a Business Structure

For any business, it is important to choose a legal business structure so that there won't be any problems with the federal department when it is time to pay taxes. You will need to choose the appropriate business structure for your business, as it may be difficult to apply for loans or manage your business in the future if you make the wrong choice.

Every country has its own regulations for business structures. Irrespective of your country's laws, business structures are usually divided into the following four types.

- **Sole Proprietorship**

A sole proprietorship is the most common and simple business structure. All the business expenses and gains will be listed as the income of the owner and hence should be filed according to these tax regulations.

Many prefer this business structure because it is inexpensive to start with and requires minimal fees to conduct business on Airbnb. The major downside, however, is that the individual will be liable for all legal issues. For example, if a guest sues you, then you will be taking complete responsibility if the court declares you guilty of their claims.

- **Partnership**

When you have two or more partners in your hosting business, it will fall into this category and should be claimed as such. Everything else from a tax perspective is similar to a sole proprietorship with this business structure.

One of the major advantages of a partnership business structure is that there will be little paperwork when compared with forming a Limited Liability Company (LLC). There are also special taxation rules that let you file a lower percentage of your income in this business structure. On the downside, just like a sole proprietorship, if something goes wrong in the business, you will be legally liable and, in the worst-case scenario, all the partners' assets can be sold off.

- **Corporation**

The corporation is the most complex but technically also the best business structure, as the tax percentage in this filing category is slightly lower. However, it is expensive to set up and hence not usually the most suitable option for Airbnb hosts.

- **Limited Liability Company**

The LLC is the most common business structure that Airbnb hosts use to handle their hosting business. It is a middle ground between the sole proprietorship and corporation business structures.

The major advantage of an LLC is that it removes liability from the owners if something goes wrong in the business. If someone sues you as the host, then legal culpability will be shifted to the LLC itself. The disadvantage here, however, is that it is expensive and it also usually requires the help of a permanent accountant to manage taxes and maintain accounts for auditing.

Which business structure should I choose?

Honestly, it is completely your choice. If you are not ready to spend the additional money on an LLC, then you can continue with a sole proprietorship. If you have co-hosts involved, then there is no choice other than to use the partnership or LLC business structure. Most of the hosts on Airbnb use an LLC as their default business structure, which makes it easy to separate their personal income from the income that is generated from their business. In addition, an LLC helps you avoid legal cases that, even though rare, can be a major headache.

Airbnb Taxes

When you are successful in any business, you will receive profits. This profit you can either save or invest further to create more wealth. While reinvesting your profits is a smart decision, you will also need to keep in mind and plan for what will be coming out for taxes each year. Every country has its own tax regulations, so if you are not aware of your tax rules or you don't trust yourself to follow them perfectly, we suggest you hire an accountant to do this work for you.

In general, in the U.S., if you rent a property for more than 14 days, you will be required to pay a part of your profits in the form of taxes to the Internal Revenue Service (IRS). You can either use Schedule C or Schedule E to report your taxes as self-employment tax.

To calculate your overall gross profit, you can use the earnings report that is provided to you by Airbnb.

1. Head over to your Airbnb account and click on the "Account Settings" option.
2. Once in the interface, look at the transaction history.
3. You can click on the gross earnings button to select a date range for the report to be generated from.
4. Once the report is generated, click on the "Download CSV" button to get your report.

What does the CSV consist of?

The CSV report that is downloaded will have a lot of information pertaining to your orders according to the dates selected.

- The date column describes the booking date of the reservation.
- The type column refers to the type of payment that was used in the transaction.
- The start date column refers to when the guest arrived at the property for their stay.
- The nights column refers to the number of nights the guest stayed on the property.
- The guests column lists the names of the guests in the reservation.
- The fees column refers to the amount of money the guest paid for the service.
- The occupancy tax refers to the tax that Airbnb collected from the hosts when the booking took place.

You can also get the tax forms you need from Airbnb itself. U.S. citizens will need to download Form 1099-K, whereas non-U.S. citizens will need to download the 1042-S form to file taxes in their country and report their gross income from hosting.

How Much Profit Can My Airbnb Property Generate?

Before investing significant resources and money into a short-term rental business with Airbnb, you need to have an idea of how much you can make with your property over the long term. You should be as realistic as possible and create goals that are achievable once you've done your research and you understand how much value you have to offer guests.

It is a hard-known fact that not all properties and localities will earn the same amount of profit, and your profit potential will largely depend on the demographics that you are targeting with your business. However, irrespective of the demographics you are targeting, you can make a decent amount of income from this business if you follow the right strategies.

You can estimate the amount of money you can earn. Remember that Airbnb charges a flat commission of 3% on all listings.

Here is a breakdown of what happens:

- Let us suppose that the guest pays $2,000 without tax to book your listing. They will also pay $200 in cleaning fees and $20 as a service fee to Airbnb for using the platform to find a place to stay.
- You will be charged $60 by Airbnb as a service fee for using their platform as a host.
- The $200 cleaning fee will be given to you without Airbnb taking any commission.
- Out of the 3% commission Airbnb has charged, you can claim 1% as an occupancy fee when filing your taxes.

To help you arrive at a reasonable estimate, you will first look up the national averages for short-term rental businesses. A popular website called Earnest.com provides private loans to students and businesses and has conducted research about the earnings related to hosting.

Here are some conclusions:

- On average, every host earns close to $1,000 in total from their property.
- It is estimated that half of Airbnb hosts have earned less than $500 from their property in their entire Airbnb career. Airbnb can be a very competitive business, and since only a few people are sharing most of the revenue pie, you should learn their success strategies and tactics. Keeping up with the strategies and tactics of successful competitors is crucial, since it's always smart to follow what's working.
- Earnest.com also estimated that for every ten hosts, one makes more than $2,000 per month, and for every thirty hosts, one makes more than $5,000 per month.

So, realistically, if you are new to the business, you need to focus on earning $2,000 per month to be considered a "successful" host in the business. However, this $2,000 can be either a gain or loss depending on the rent you are paying or the amount of money you are spending on the property and maintenance.

Conducting Market and Area Research

For any business, you need to conduct market and area research to make smart business choices. Investing your capital without any research is a bad idea because you need to see the path forward as clearly as possible, lest you risk making mistakes where you could have had a plan in place.

Let us suppose that you have listed a property on Airbnb and are earning $1,000 per month. You have checked what others are making from similar listings and have concluded that they are making $500 per month on average in your locality. You would feel good about yourself in this scenario because you are making more than double what your competition is making.

But what if your competitors are making $2,000 per month and you are only bringing in half as much? You might be devastated because you are not making as much as you could, so you find ways to improve the value of what you are offering. Understanding the competition market and the area is important to understand whether or not you are likely to be successful.

Included in your research should be an adequate amount of data with statistics. You can use online resources to get this data for your research. Even though this data is public, you may need to pay a fee to access it, as the data can be filtered according to your requirements.

What data should I pay attention to?

To get a big picture understanding of a market or a locality where you are keen to start your Airbnb business, you need to look at the parameters I've described below while conducting your research.

Daily Rates

You need to look at the nightly rates for area properties to get a good estimation of what guests are willing to pay for staying in those Airbnb listings. While there will be cheap options and luxurious options, you need to calculate the median for the nightly rates and either bump or reduce your listing price accordingly depending on what you are expecting the profit margins to be.

How do I research daily rates?

1. Head over to Airdna.com and log in to your premium account. You need to purchase a premium account to access this data.
2. In the dashboard, you can click on "Research and Analysis" for a new interface to open up.
3. You can now select the type of graph you want to use to display the data and then select the different data available. Select the "Daily Rates" option.
4. In the same interface, choose the location and adjust the dates for which you want to search.
5. Once this is done, click on the "Apply" button for results to pop up.
6. You can now look at the daily rates data via different graphs to understand how daily rates have impacted bookings for your competitors.

Occupancy Rates

You will also need to research occupancy rates during the year to see the patterns that emerge. This will give you a good idea of the busy and dull seasons. Knowing about these occupancy rates for similar listings in your area will help you prepare for the busy season as well as be ready to reduce your nightly rates when the low season approaches.

How do I research occupancy rates?

1. Head over to Airdna.com and log in to your premium account.
2. In the dashboard, you can click on "Research and Analysis" for a new interface to open up. Select the "Occupancy Rates" option.
3. In the same interface, choose the location and adjust the dates for which you want to filter.
4. Once this is done, click on the "Apply" button for results to pop up.
5. In the results, you can look at how occupancy rates have changed for different seasons.

Rental Revenue

It is also important to know how many hosts are actually making a profit from their Airbnb businesses in the relevant area. While data between the years 2020 and 2021 can be demotivating due to the lockdown restrictions imposed, you can check the years before that to see how things might rebound as the economy moves back to normal.

How do I research rental revenue?

1. Visit pricelabs.com and log in to your premium account.
2. You can now look at the dashboard and select the "Revenue Research" option.
3. In the next interface, provide your location details and the years for which you want to filter the data for short-term rentals in your location.
4. Click on the "Download" button to download a CSV file.
5. Open it with Microsoft Excel and find out whether the overall revenue for rentals has increased or

decreased in your location to have a better understanding of the host business.

What further research can I do?

To understand the statistics and make your research much more helpful, you need to dive into several other factors that we will discuss below. To access all the data you need, you should use tools such as Airdna.

Open your premium account at Airdna and click on the "Advanced Research" option in the dashboard. You can then filter the data for several statistics mentioned below according to your requirements. Enter the location and desired dates for the data to be as precise as possible for your research.

- **Market Mix**

The term "market mix" describes how listings perform based on their location and potential guest demographics. For example, you may need to find the statistics for urban and rural listings to judge how they are performing according to their locality.

Knowing the respective performance data of different sub-lists can give you a more rounded understanding of the Airbnb market.

- **Long-Term Trends**

It can be misleading to analyze your findings just by looking at short-term trends. You need to look at the last 10 years' worth of statistics to more accurately assess whether listings like yours do well over the long term. If stats are trending up for your type of listing, then you are looking good regarding your investment. If not, then try to figure out the reasons for why profits are decreasing over the long term.

- **Amenities Statistics**

You need to analyze information regarding amenities to ensure that your listing offers what people tend to look for in your target demographics, especially if you are just starting out and creating your new listing. Compare your listing with the top listings in your area on the Airbnb website to figure out what you may be missing and what you can highlight as unique to your property. Don't forget to include the basics that are offered everywhere else. It is common for hosts to provide things like coffee/coffeemaker, towels, etc.

- **Future Statistics**

Several services such as Airdna and Pricelabs use advanced machine learning and data analysis algorithms to estimate future prices and occupancy rates for listings in a particular area or category. You can make use of these statistics to set your prices for different seasons.

- **Top Listings**

Learn what the top Airbnb listings are doing right by collecting information about them on the Airbnb website. When you understand what the top performers are doing to be successful, you will be able to make better decisions and customizations to increase your revenue.

- **Rating Statistics**

Analyzing how guests have rated properties in a locality or an area can help you understand your guest demographics in a better way. If you are in an area where guests are mostly dissatisfied, then you need to be extra careful and should provide additional amenities. The dissatisfied reviews can help you improve your listings so that future guests won't have to deal with these issues at your properties.

Competition Analysis

While analyzing market statistics is a quick and easy process, you do, however, need to understand your competition in detail to improve your business. Competition analysis can help you understand the strategies and tactics that successful hosts in your locality are using to ensure that they win more bookings. Competition analysis will give you a clear picture of what is working and what is not for a host.

To analyze the competition, first research and choose the top performing listings in your locality or area. It doesn't make sense to include a comparison of all the listings because every locality has its own set of rules.

How do I analyze competition using Airdna?

Head over to Airdna.com and open your dashboard. Once in the dashboard, select the "Competition Analysis" option. In the next interface, select your location and dates on the toolbar to generate the listings of your competitors. Depending on your location, these results will vary from less than 10 listings to sometimes up to hundreds of competitor listings.

Manually select the top 10 or 20 listings and compare the below-mentioned parameters on your own or use a comparison tool such as Mashvisor to review the averages. You will be using this data while creating your listing.

- Check the rent that competitors are charging for a single day.
- Check the management fees they are charging.
- Check the utilities they are providing for guests.
- Check whether or not they are providing additional amenities such as satellite, cable, and/or massage chairs.
- Check how they are handling cleaning and what fees they are charging the guests.
- Check how frequently they are repairing or performing maintenance on their property. To get these statistics, you can use short-term rental statistics that are usually released by the U.S. housing department.
- Check what permits the listings are using. You can contact your local city office to find out what permits these listings have. The information is public and can be accessed by anyone.

Understanding Your Airbnb Expenses

Before starting the process of creating your listing, you need to have a rough estimate of your upfront costs to get started. Hosting on Airbnb is not a business that you can start without any capital. In many cases, hosts will need to spend some money to prepare their investment to be successful on Airbnb. Without enough investment money upfront, it will be difficult for you to prepare your property for this very competitive market.

How much do I need to start?

First of all, if you have a property to host, then your upfront investment will include considerations for amenities and marketing costs. If you don't have a property, then you will need to rent or lease a property. The rates for renting different properties will vary depending on the demand and the locality.

You may also need to consider having a co-host if you don't have enough money to get things off the ground. Once the property is decided on, you may need to furnish each room, and this might cost up to $2,000 for every room in the property to be furnished with basic amenities.

Total Calculation:

Let us suppose that you have a property with six rooms and are trying to host the property on Airbnb. An approximate cost analysis is shown below with a complete breakdown.

- $12,000 to $15,000 for furnishing all the rooms with basic amenities.
- $1,000 to $1,500 for a professional photographer to take photos for your listing.
- A minimum of $1,000 for virtual assistants if you want to automate your work.
- A minimum of $1,000 to purchase an electronic lock and smart lock for your listing.
- A minimum of $500 to buy automated tools and software, which either have a one-time fee or a subscription fee depending on what they do. These

tools can help you manage your Airbnb account or handle your guest communications effectively.
- If you are making an agreement with a property management company to manage your cleaning and other tasks associated with the process, then you will need to pay an upfront fee of at least $2,000.

When you add up all of these costs, the starting expense for a medium-sized Airbnb property will be anywhere from $20,000 to $25,000. Once you start earning profits in the business, you can reinvest to purchase additional amenities to improve on your property.

If you don't have a property, then you could be looking at an additional $25,000 to $50,000 needed for the initial months as an investment to rent a property that allows you to host the property online.

Insurance

You need to protect yourself from any liability should something unfortunate take place during a time when you have a guest staying on your property. You don't want to be in a situation where you aren't insured and have to pay out of pocket for these incidents, as it can really dig you into a hole. Even though Airbnb provides its own insurance, we suggest you look at other channels as discussed below.

Why is it important to be insured?

Insurance provides you with financial security if something unfortunate happens at your property. In a business, it is always important to consider risk management to minimize losses, and insurance is one of those things that you really need to think about while hosting using Airbnb. Insurance eliminates the risks associated with issues such as property damage or injury to guests, even if you have taken all the required steps to create a safe environment. Insurance can usually help hosts in the worst-case scenarios.

Airbnb's Liability Protection

Airbnb provides mandatory $1 million insurance for all the hosts who list their property on the Airbnb website. Using this policy, you can claim money up to $1 million for damages that occur because of a guest staying on your property.

It's great protection for hosts, as Airbnb will often link you with a third-party insurance firm that will handle all the procedures when you make a claim regarding an issue. Apart from the $1 million insurance, hosts will also have an additional layer of security because of Airbnb's host protection policy. You will be covered for any damage caused by guests to your property, unexpected cleaning costs, or canceled bookings due to the actions of the guests.

Even though Airbnb's liability protection is great for hosts, you should not completely rely on it due to the following reasons.

- One of the primary reasons is that it doesn't provide you with complete control. When you submit a claim, Airbnb must first verify and claim it to the insurance firm. If they don't accept it, then you may not get paid at all for your damages. Due to an additional layer of an intermediary, the process becomes much more complicated than it looks on paper.

- Airbnb is fundamentally a company, and therefore they are careful about having too many claims in a financial year. If there is an increase in the number of claims, then this directly increases the premiums that need to be paid to the firm. For many reasons, Airbnb may choose to end some claims.

Buying Your Own Insurance for Full Protection

To ensure that you are fully protected for any unforeseen circumstances, we suggest you purchase your own liability insurance for your properties that are listed on Airbnb. This provides three-layer protection:

1. The first line of defense will be the security deposit that you collect from the guest.
2. The second line of defense will be the liability policy that is provided for hosts by Airbnb.
3. The third line of defense will be your own liability insurance plan.

How do I purchase my own liability policy?

To start, we suggest you reach out to a broker among your local independent companies. While there are online insurance companies in business, it is still recommended to first approach brokers from your locality to help you with choosing the right insurance policy according to the property that you are insuring.

The premium that needs to be paid will also depend on the level of protection that you are expecting from the policy. Your local crime rate may also have an effect on the premium that needs to be paid. Most of the time, a host will choose protection of between $100k and $1 million from individual policies they take.

Tip:

To find brokers in your locality, do a quick Google search or ask for referrals in your neighborhood. You can also look for brokers in various Facebook groups for Airbnb hosts. Most of the time, you won't need to pay anything for the brokers, as all of them will receive a commission from the insurance firms themselves.

Airbnb Regulations

As Airbnb started to evolve, governments began putting different regulations in place around them. As they fall under the short-term rentals category, you need to also be aware of the relevant regulatory rules to ensure that you are not doing anything illegal in your area.

Some of the things hosts can get into trouble for include:

- not having an eligible license
- not following the local rules, such as hosting without a parking space
- having your property near a school or hospital
- having your property close to an army warehouse

It is quite impossible to list all the regulations that might pertain to an area, and therefore we recommend that you do your own research or contact a tax professional to learn about your local regulations. Airbnb will also send you emails that ask you to check the city rules before listing on Airbnb.

Not following regulations can have serious consequences. Most of the time it will result in you paying hefty fines, but you can even land in jail if there is any physical damage to the guests due to you not following safety regulations. Not knowing the regulation laws can result in you losing your profits for many reasons, so knowing and following these rules is essential to building a successful hosting business.

What are the risks of not following regulations?

Both local and country-wide regulations are becoming more and more hostile toward short-term rentals. While this may be concerning for people like you who are interested in hosting their properties, we also need to understand the perspective of governments. Cases have been discovered in which individuals were using short-term rentals as a way to launder their money, and so more severe punishments are being imposed by law enforcement. They are also doing more thorough checks to look for any signs of illegal activity.

Following are some of the factors that demonstrate how local regulations can impact your profit potential.

- **Licensing**

Initially, there were no license restrictions for Airbnb properties. These days, however, some city authorities around the country are allowing only a limited number of properties to be licensed and listed as Airbnb rental properties. In some of these cities, you need to first apply and pay for the license so that you can list your property legally before guests can stay there. Sometimes these authorities will also allow properties from only certain localities of the city. If there are no available licenses, then you may need to wait for a few months before the next license slots open up. Slots usually open up every three months in metropolitan cities and once every six months for rural areas.

While the regulations were loosened a bit due to the COVID pandemic, which hugely affected the hospitality business in recent years, it is believed that the rules will be more strictly enforced in the coming years.

- **Fines**

Fines for operating an illegal listing can destroy not only your Airbnb business but also your personal finances. For example, last year, a San Francisco couple was fined more than $2 million dollars for operating 14 illegal Airbnb listings, and it's not just the U.S. In other countries, including France and the U.K., they are enforcing huge fines to combat illegal activities that are surging in the Airbnb properties.

- **Revenue Potential**

The local regulations and laws can ultimately dictate whether or not your listing will be a profitable venture for you. For example, if the local laws allow only 120 days per year on a license for short-term rental properties, then you need to calculate whether or not you can make enough profit in this time frame to make the business viable in your area.

Learn About Restrictions

The laws and regulations will vary based on the property you own and where it is located. While professionals can do this research for you, their services might cost you a fortune. Doing your own research might be a good idea, especially if you are just starting with your Airbnb business. Once you start to lease more properties as part of your business, you can hire a professional to do the research for different areas and regulations.

- **Airbnb Help Center**

Airbnb itself provides extensive guides for hosts to learn about and understand what they are getting into. The Airbnb help center is a great place to begin searching for these details. Visit the "Help Center" page and enter the name of your city to learn about the local regulations.

- **Search Engines**

Search engines such as Google can help you find comprehensive details about any queries you may have with regard to regulations and laws. You can use keywords such as "regulations," "short-term rentals," and "Airbnb property laws" to find meaningful information that is specific to your questions.

- **Local Hosting Groups**

You might join your local Airbnb host groups on Facebook or Meetup to talk to other hosts and see how they are dealing with regulations. Most of the hosts in these groups will be willing to help you without charging a fee. You do, however, need to get approval from the administrators to join some of the groups, and some others are open for anyone to join. Once you are accepted, you can post questions about regulations.

- **City Hall Website and Offices**

All cities maintain records related to commercial and housing property rules to help their citizens, and these are kept in municipal offices. You can either visit the official website or call them during working hours to ask about the latest rules for short-term rental properties. If you do not get sufficient information this way, then you can visit the city hall office personally to learn about these laws and regulations from the officials themselves.

Chapter 3

Preparing Your Airbnb Property

Preparing your Airbnb property to be ready to host guests is not an easy task. It is not just about placing a bed in your room and making your list live for guests to come and stay on your property. While this may work for cheap hotel services, Airbnb is not a cheap option, and a lot of guests expect the best out of their stays. As a host, you need to focus carefully on details regarding furnishing, decorating, and equipping your properties with the most commonly desired amenities.

As a host, you also need to focus on managing in a way that impacts and improves your profit potential for your business. For example, if you increase your nightly rate by just $10 extra, you could be making $3,650 more in profits over the course of the year. However, it is important to justify the increase in price per night by creating a stay experience that goes above and beyond other listings in your area.

There are three important steps to making sure that guests will have a good experience at your property:

- Ensure that the property is ready and that it has all required amenities that you included in the description of your listing.
- Make sure that you are committed to providing a five-star experience to your guests, regardless of the hurdles you may face.
- Form a good relationship with either your landlord or neighbors.

Realistic Expectations

As someone who has experience with Airbnb hosting, we often stress the fact that all hosts should maintain realistic expectations about the profit potential of their listing. For example, in a locality like Idaho, it is probably not possible to earn $3,000 per month from your property, even if you offer lots of great amenities in a spotless home. You need to understand the demographics that are in line with your potential guests who might want to visit your locality. On the other hand, in an area like Brooklyn, it is quite easy to earn more than $5,000 per month even if you provide minimal amenities. This is because there are so many people keen to rent spaces for many different work or vacation activities there. As New York is a hotspot for businesses and tourists, hosts there can usually ask a higher nightly rate for guests to stay at their property.

Study your demographics and optimize your pricing, then you can begin the process of setting up your amenities and optimizing your space. We'll go over what to do for this step in the next section.

Optimizing Your Space

Regardless of how big your property is, you need to find a way to optimize the space and provide high value to your guests. Each property has its own potential, and your primary goal should be to maximize that potential.

Spending more time on optimizing your space can lead to positive reviews and higher levels of satisfaction from your guests, helping you to earn more profits in the long run. While the initial investment may be higher to create a well-thought-out experience for your guests, the results will be worth it, especially if you are offering a luxurious experience with all the desired amenities provided.

Quick Tips to Maximize Your Listing Potential

- **Never block off rooms.**

Sometimes hosts block off a room because construction is not yet completed or because they use the room as a personal space. While you may have your reasons to lock a room, it is highly recommended that you do not do it. Guests might become disappointed if they find out that they can't use a space that they thought was part of the property for their use.

- **Ensure that the sleeping arrangements are top notch.**

Make sure that the sleeping amenities provided by you are comfortable for the guest. Many hosts make the mistake of placing a king-size bed in a room which directly reduces the free space that is available. While a king-size bed can be luxurious, it can still make a space feel congested, and this could lead to negative reviews. Optimization is not just focusing on providing the best and costliest amenities but also ensuring that your guests have a comfortable amount of space to easily move around or relax on the property.

- **Focus more on decoration.**

Decoration and aesthetics not only provide a unique look for your listing but will also help you to attract more attention from potential guests as they are browsing through properties. Small touches like having a small coffee cup and a flower pot in the right place can make a huge difference from an aesthetic point of view. As Gen Z and millennial guests tend to focus more on how things look, it is important to consider these things while optimizing your space.

Getting Started

There is always room for an upgrade in the Airbnb business, but you should first focus on the basic amenities that are essential to most guests. Over time, and as you get more bookings, you can begin to spend a portion of your profits on improving the stay experience that you provide to your guests.

Start with a minimal nightly rate that includes basic amenities that you can provide for your guests. You don't need to upgrade your bed from a queen to a king right away. Don't stress about spending lots of money on amenities right away, especially if you are new to the Airbnb business. Optimize what you can offer right now to create a solid initial offering. You can build on this as you grow.

There are certain amenities that guests will expect to be part of your listing. Avoid any luxurious items initially, as they can reduce your return on investment. You may, however, spend money on a 4K TV or a high-end appliance after a few bookings to expand the amenities offered in your listing.

What Amenities Do Guests Expect?

As a host, you need to have a clear idea of what amenities guests will expect from your listing. One of the better ways to learn what amenities your guests will be expecting in your locality is to glance through the positive reviews of listings in your area. Look at those reviews and see what amenities guests tend to mention in their reviews. If they are mentioning them specifically in their reviews, it means that they were impressed with the amenities, and this tells you that they are non-negotiables that will likely boost your listing ranking.

Types of Amenities for Your Listing

In Airbnb properties, the most important amenities that guests care about are furniture and appliances. All other amenities you provide might wow them, but they may become difficult to maintain, especially if you are not actively following your return on investment regarding those amenities.

Must-have amenities are important and mandatory for your Airbnb business to thrive. Upgraded amenities, on the other hand, will wow your customer and improve your chances for more positive reviews after their stay.

Before looking at the below-mentioned amenities, take a piece of paper and a pen and brainstorm the amenities that come immediately to your mind. Once you write them down, divide them and place them into four different columns: must-have amenities, nice-to-have amenities, outstanding amenities, and waste-of-money amenities.

How do I choose amenities?

Just like any other part of the business, it is important to do research before furnishing your space with amenities. We suggest you check out your competitors' listings to reassess what amenities will be ideal for your guests. You can use research tools to determine which listings are performing better and take note of all the amenities they are providing to their guests. We have provided a list of tools that Airbnb hosts use at the end of this book. Take a look at those for a better idea of what popular tools are available to you.

It is also important to research amenities according to the size of your listing. It is counterproductive to research listings that are very large or much smaller than your space, as you will not be able to use a similar set of options.

Must-Have Amenities

Listed below are amenities that you should provide for your guests without any problems so that they have an enjoyable stay. These are essential to earn positive reviews for your property and you as a host.

- **Bed**

Your guests need to have someplace to sleep, and these spaces should be a priority as you make preparations. Ensure that each bed and mattress are of high quality. You might also provide an air mattress and a sleeper sofa as complementary benefits for your guests.

- **Clean Towels and Sheets**

Both of these things are essential for your guest stays. Perfectly clean sheets make a good first impression on your guests. Most guests will be irked if they see unclean towels or sheets in their rooms. Provide not just one towel but a couple of towels for each guest that stays on your property.

- **Coffee Maker**

Coffee is a popular beverage and hence a must-have for many guests who will visit your listing. It is a good idea to provide them with at least a basic coffee maker, as this will provide a home-like feeling for most guests.

- **Well-Equipped Kitchen**

The kitchen is one of the most important places to focus on when preparing your listing. Ensure that there are plates, cups, spatulas, and pans for your guests to use if they want to cook for themselves. Provide a good, reliable stove and gas connection, too. As most guests are usually not keen to travel for every meal, having a well-equipped kitchen can help them experience a more comfortable stay.

Recommended tools for the kitchen include the following:

- cups and dishes
- knives, forks, and spoons
- pots and pans

- spatulas
- chopping boards
- baking supplies
- spice rack

- **A Good Refrigerator**

A refrigerator is a mandatory appliance that you need to provide for your guests. Provide water bottles inside the fridge along with a small manual so that your guests can operate it without any hiccups.

- **Microwave**

It is important to provide a microwave for guests to heat their food, such as leftovers or takeout. A small one should suffice for this purpose. You can also invest in a larger one if the property is designed to accommodate a large family.

- **Water**

It is essential that you provide clean water 24/7 for your guests. Ensure that the water is safe to drink and tastes good. Not providing clean water will be a huge turn-off for most guests.

- **Wi-Fi**

No matter where your guests come from, they will often want to connect to the outside world via the internet. International data charges can be higher, and so it is your responsibility to provide high-speed Wi-Fi to all your guests.

- **Bathroom Amenities**

Leaving enough bathroom amenities for your guests, such as toilet paper, hand towels, and tissues, is also mandatory. Only leaving enough toilet paper for the first few hours is not a good idea. Sometimes there are issues with guests stealing toilet paper in some cases. However, you need to understand that it is worth losing 10 dollars to make most of your compliant guests happy. You shouldn't disappoint the guests who just want to have a comfortable stay.

Recommended bathroom amenities include the following:

- shampoo/conditioner
- bodywash
- bathroom hooks
- towel racks
- hair dryer
- air freshener

Additional Amenities

Ensure that you are furnishing the property with other basic amenities, such as a curtain for the shower, working sinks, and running hot water for whenever your guests need it.

The Often Forgotten

There are some basic amenities that lots of hosts forget to include on their property. Here is a list of some of them for your convenience:

- A bedside table with a lamp. A lot of guests need to place their spectacles somewhere, or sometimes they want to read a book before sleeping. Providing them with a cheap table and lamp from IKEA, at minimum, is a good idea.

- We recommend placing some natural or artificial plants inside the space. However, don't over-furnish the property with plants, as some guests might be irritated by excess greenery.
- Ensure that you provide sharp knives, as this is a basic requirement for cooking.
- Provide common spices, salts, and cooking oil to ensure that your guests will be able to cook without any hassle.

Nice-to-Have Amenities

There are some amenities that hosts can offer that fall under the nice-to-have category. Take a look at the following list for some ideas:

- A dishwasher is not necessarily a mandatory amenity that you need to provide, but it can win you lots of brownie points from your guests.
- A smart TV will usually fall under the nice-to-have amenities. If you decide to include one, ensure that it supports HDR resolution. Provide a streaming device such as Apple TV or Google Chromecast for guests to watch any of their favorite shows or films while staying cozy in their bed. As most guests watch Netflix shows, it is suggested that you provide a Netflix account for your guests.
- You can improve the quality of your coffee maker or provide guests with an espresso machine to go the extra mile.

- Provide wine glasses for guests to enjoy their alcohol while having a romantic date with their partner.
- Provide a toaster oven as a nice additional option for your guests when they are not in the mood for cooking.

Outstanding Amenities

The best amenities are those that you spend a little extra on to ensure that your guests have a wonderful stay. These amenities will provide satisfaction and can even win you repeat guests who might make staying with you an annual tradition.

The following are some examples of amenities that would fall in this category:

- universal mobile chargers and plugs so that international guests can easily charge their smartphones and laptops
- high-quality speakers along with your smart TV so that guests can enjoy their favorite movies or TV shows with a good Dolby Atmos experience
- entertainment systems such as gaming consoles–this can be a great idea, especially if you are hosting a younger demographic of large families, as they are usually more inclined to play games
- a laptop-friendly workspace for your guests
- a foosball table for your guests to have some fun with their friends and family

Warning:

There is always the chance that guests will steal your mobile chargers or the games that are provided for them. Be sure to always verify that these items are present and intact before and after each check-out and if necessary, require a suitable security deposit to cover the loss should expensive amenities be damaged or stolen.

How do I avoid wasting money?

There are some amenities that many hosts waste their money on. While these amenities might provide a good impression for guests, their costs could reduce your profit potential.

Consider the following as examples:

- A massage chair is one of the unnecessary amenities that hosts might spend their money on. They cost anywhere from $15,000 to $25,000, even for a basic one.
- High-end satellite TV connection is another amenity that hosts spend more money on than is usually necessary. As you are already providing Wi-Fi and local cable connection, it doesn't make sense from a business perspective to spend a couple hundred dollars every month on this amenity.

Guest Manual

Guests usually have general queries related to logging into Wi-Fi or how to operate the thermostat on the property. While you can help each guest with the answers to these queries, you can simplify the process by providing pre-written instructions so you don't have to repeat yourself every time you book a guest.

Providing instructions is also a safe way to make sure that all the electrical appliances you are providing are used correctly.

Include the most commonly asked questions and place hard copies of this guide on the property so that the guests will not face any problem trying to access the manual digitally.

In the next section, we will highlight some common information that guests tend to ask hosts about.

- **Instructions for Accessing Wi-Fi**

Wi-Fi is the most important amenity that guests usually ask about when they visit a listing. It is recommended that you provide a QR code so guests can easily scan it and instantly connect to the Wi-Fi without entering any password. To get the QR code for your Wi-Fi, you can check the router settings using the IP address 192.168.0.1 and log in with your credentials. There will be a separate section called "Sharing" from which you can generate a QR code and print it on paper for your guests to scan with their phones. You may also send this code through the chat so guests will have it in advance.

- **Parking Information**

When you send the digital guide for your listing, you should highlight the information about where they can park their vehicles. Not all listings have garages or parking spaces, so you should provide clear instructions about the space you have allotted near your listing for parking. Instead of just saying "park in front of the white building," the guide should provide clear instructions about how to approach the white building.

- **Highlight Pet and Family Policies**

In the guide, it is important to provide information about the restrictions that you have in place for pets and kids at the property.

Consider the following:

- Provide information about the pet food that has been provided and where they can find it.
- Provide details about the amenities that you have provided specifically for kids.
- Provide instructions about the rooms where fire extinguishers and carbon monoxide alarms are present to ensure the safety of the guests.

Be sure to include a step-by-step guide for amenities. It is also important that you provide information about all essentials that are provided on your property.

Examples:

- "You can find the thermostat on the wall. Turn it left to adjust the temperature. You can also look at the temperature that you have set on the digital screen beside it."
- "Please ensure that nothing goes inside the toilet except for toilet paper."
- "All the dishes and essential oils are provided in the cabin. On the first floor, there are spices, salts, and pepper for your use. On the second rack in the kitchen, you will find the plates and pans for cooking."
- "You can place the trash in the first bin in the living room. Please do not take the trash outside."

- "Please use the water consciously and make sure that you turn off the water tap before leaving."

Apart from the amenities, you also need to provide instructions for all appliances included in the guide.

Examples:

- "Switch on the smart TV by clicking on the power button on the side. You can then use the remote provided to access any channels. You can also connect any HDMI-supported device using the port provided."
- "You can use the PS4 console provided. Just click the 'PS' button on the joystick for the console to start. There are three games available for you on the table to have some fun during your stay."

While writing instructions in the guide, ensure that you are providing them in simple English. Not all guests will know English as their first language, so you need to be as concise as possible. If you receive more international guests, then it may be a good idea to translate the guide to other common languages such as Chinese, Japanese, and Spanish.

Creating House Rules

Setting down house rules is important when you are inviting guests into your property. Without any house rules, it becomes extremely difficult to manage your property because the guests will not be aware of what to do and what not to do. Airbnb encourages all hosts to provide host rules to avoid having to deal with any unfortunate circumstances.

I've provided a list of house rules that you may want to use. House rules will often need to be customized according to your property. You also need to provide hard copies of these rules for your guests when they enter the property to ensure that they are aware of the rules and that they will not cause any problems by not following them.

Where Do House Rules Go?

When you are creating a listing on the Airbnb app or website, there is a special section called "House Rules" where you need to add this so that Airbnb can list these rules specifically when guests are trying to book your property. If you don't post the rules in this section, then it will become hard to enforce rules by yourself, as guests are usually not aware of these rules before committing to stay on your property. For example, if pets are not allowed on your property, and they are not aware of these rules before arriving, then it will be difficult to convince them and could lead to bad reviews.

Some house rules to enforce on your property should include the following:

- Strictly state that no parties are allowed for the guests. Even if guests assure you that they will be quiet and won't damage anything, it is better to not allow parties on your property. If you decide to allow parties during the low season, then make sure that the rule is deleted from the house rules section.
- Make a strict rule about how many guests can be allowed inside the property. If more guests stay than were agreed upon, write down how much extra they need to pay for each additional individual.

- Add a strict "No Smoking" rule to your list. Smoking is quite common with guests, but we suggest not allowing guests to smoke on your property.
- Clearly state the quiet hours while they are staying on the property. During these hours, guests should keep noise to a minimum.
- Write down the rules regarding pets if your landlord is not interested in pets making messes on the property. Only a few people travel with their pets, so it will probably not affect your business too much if you enforce a strict no-pet policy. During the low season, however, you should consider lifting these rules so that you have more potential bookings coming in.

In the rules section, also write what will happen if the guests break any of the rules. For example, explicitly state that if guests host a party on the property, they are violating the rules and will lose 100% of their security deposit as a penalty.

How do I enforce these rules?

Enforcing rules can be tough, especially if you are not communicating well with your guests. In order to charge guests money for disobeying the rules, you must first resolve the issue peacefully.

- First of all, contact the guest and inform them that they are breaking the rules. Communicate to them in a polite manner and warn them that there will be penalties if they deviate from the rules again.
- If you are unable to resolve the issue, you must rely on Airbnb's mediation process to ensure that the

guests receive all the information they need regarding how they have violated the rules. Send photos whenever needed and contact the support team. The team will try their best to contact the guest and enforce charges for any damages they have caused.

Communication with Neighbors

The Airbnb business can be challenging because you also need to communicate with your neighbors and landlords. You don't want to cause them headaches or let them face problems because of the guests that arrive at your property every few days. A good host will maintain good relationships with their neighbors and landlords so that they feel comfortable reaching out to you if there are any problems that need to be resolved.

In a business like hosting on Airbnb, you need neighbors as your allies to help you keep an eye on your guests. On the other hand, having neighbors who disturb your guests is also not an ideal situation for running your Airbnb business.

How to Be a Good Neighbor

Being a good neighbor is to understand the possible stress that they may face due to guests coming and going from your property all the time. It is important to feel comfortable communicating with them about these concerns personally. The house rules should be designed to maintain your neighbors' comfort and privacy as well as your own. For example, if you allow guests to host a party, then it is likely that this will disturb your neighbors. Now you've got disgruntled neighbors holding a grudge against you, and the next time they may call the police instead of talking to you, adding to your own stress load.

For a good relationship with your neighbors, you need to have a line of communication and positive rapport with them. Be honest and help them understand that you are doing all you can to make sure guests are abiding by the rules and not disturbing the peace around the property. The following are some tips for managing neighbor relationships:

- Give them your contact information and say that they are welcome to call you if there is any problem due to your guests.
- Tell them about your schedule and when you will be available to fix any of the issues that they have raised.
- Let them know about the property management companies or cleaners that you have hired to manage your listing while you are physically away from the property.

Maintain a Good Relationship with Your Landlord

Dealing with your landlord is another important relationship, as you are essentially renting their property and listing it on Airbnb. We do not recommend hosting without consent from your landlord. Some landlords are strictly against hosting their properties using Airbnb. You need to create a proper lease agreement and tell them that you intend to use the property for a short-term rental business. Listing without proper consent can lead to unfortunate consequences, such as your landlord evicting your guests from the property. This would directly spoil your reputation and certainly earn bad reviews.

How to Pitch to Landlords

- It is important to have good communication skills when letting landlords know why hosting is important for you. Use the following tips to help them understand the opportunities that come with listing the property on Airbnb.
- Share your listing details with your landlord so that they can see how you are maintaining the property for hosting guests. Be transparent during this process.
- Explain to them in detail how hosting can help you earn additional income and allow you to rent the property for longer periods of time.
- Tell them that you will be covering any services that may be needed on the property while you are listing it on Airbnb.
- Let them know about the $1 million liability insurance that Airbnb provides for any damages that may be caused by the guests.
- Pay rent in advance, and pay a bigger security deposit so that they are more likely to feel comfortable with you hosting using Airbnb.

Choosing a Cancellation Policy

Airbnb is famous with guests around the world due to its accommodating and convenient cancellation policy. As a host, you need to be aware of six different cancellation policies that are offered by Airbnb and why we recommend going with the stricter policy as a host.

What are the Six Cancellation Policies?

While publicizing your listing, you need to select from the following six cancellation policies. You need to be aware that Airbnb will be constantly monitoring and may change policy details. If you want to stay on top of the game, don't forget to read the newsletters provided by Airbnb whenever there are any new changes implemented. All the newsletters will be sent to your Airbnb-registered email address.

- **Flexible**

This is the most convenient cancellation policy for guests. They can cancel their bookings 24 hours before the check-in time and will get a full refund, including both the nightly rate and cleaning fees that they have paid. They will not receive the service fee as a refund.

- **Moderate**

In a moderate cancellation policy, the guests are allowed to cancel five days before the check-in and can get a full refund apart from the service fee that has been charged.

- **Strict**

In a strict cancellation policy, the guests can only cancel seven days prior to the check-in and will receive only 50% of the nightly rate and cleaning fee they have paid. The service fee will not be refunded.

- **Long-Term Bookings**

Hosts may lose potential income because of long-term bookings, which typically last longer than 30 days, so they may have strict cancellation policies in place. If a long-term booking is canceled, it may be difficult for hosts to find new guests to replace them. The guest can cancel even on the day of check-in but will only receive a refund for anything past 30 days. Let's suppose that the guest booked your property for 60 days and canceled. The first 30 days' worth of fees do not need to be refunded, but the remaining 30 days' worth of fees must be refunded. The service fee will not be refunded.

- **Super Strict 30 Days**

This cancellation policy is often used by the most popular listings in a locality. Superhosts can also use this model to avoid unpromising bookings from guests. With this policy, guests can receive 50% of the nightly rate and cleaning fee as a refund if the booking is canceled 30 days before check-in. Airbnb invites you to use this cancellation policy if you are an eligible host. The service fee will not be refunded.

- **Super Strict 60 Days**

This cancellation policy is allowed for only the most popular listings in the country. It is available to superhosts who have consistent bookings and positive ratings. With this policy, guests need to cancel their booking at least 60 days before check-in to receive a 50% refund of the nightly rate and cleaning fee. Airbnb will send an invitation if you become eligible for this cancellation policy. The service fee will not be refunded.

What do I choose?

If you are new to the business, then we suggest you explore the flexible cancellation policy, as it will be easier to get your initial bookings for your listing. With time, however, you need to explore a stricter cancellation policy to safeguard your bookings and avoid dealing with constant cancellations, which will result in a decrease in your profits.

Chapter 4

Listing Your Airbnb Property

To win the attention from guests who are browsing different options provided to them on the Airbnb website or app, you need to optimize several areas of your listing. We will provide info about all of them to help you improve your search rankings in less time for your locality. Before learning about the different aspects you need to focus on while creating a listing, let us show you first how to create a listing as a host.

Creating a Listing

1. To list a property on Airbnb, you need to first create an account with them. Head over to airbnb.com/signup to create an account with either your mobile number or email address.
2. In your profile section, click on the host option and click to create a listing.

3. When you create a new listing, you will need to fill in different fields before your listing can go live on the Airbnb website.

The Importance of a Strong Headline

The headline is the most crucial part of your listing. It is essentially the first thing that guests will notice while glancing through dozens or even hundreds of other listings, alongside a cover photo. You need to create a strong headline to attract the attention of your potential guests.

You shouldn't, however, be deceptive with false promises in your headline just to attract viewers, as this will reduce your conversion rate even when lots of people are clicking on your listing. Conversion rate refers to the percentage of how many guests actually book your property after they see your listing. While writing a headline, be truthful and honestly capture what you are offering to guests in words. Before writing your headline, brainstorm what your future guests will expect and create a perfect listing headline. You may initially glance through your competition's headlines to get an idea of what a good headline looks like.

Essentials to Writing a Great Headline

Writing headlines for a business is usually called "copywriting" in the business world. Copywriting is a professional job, and if you want to hire someone to write headlines for you, by all means. However, if you are a beginner, it doesn't make sense to spend thousands of dollars on a professional copywriter.

Anyone can write a good headline with a little bit of research on the demographics. Your primary goal needs to be appealing to the potential guests that may be interested in your listing.

Ask yourself the question while writing a headline, "Why do people want to book my listing? What do they desire from my listing?" When you try to find answers to these questions, you will usually start to think about some of the following information.

- Guests usually want to know about the main accommodations, such as the number of bedrooms and bathrooms that the listing provides.
- Guests usually want to learn about the locality of the property.
- Guests want to see the mood of the property where they are going to stay. Some properties can be minimalistic while others are more aesthetic.
- Guests like to check out what events or restaurants are close by as they visualize their stay.

You need to try to mention all or at least some of these details while writing your headline.

For example, "A great property near the airport" is not a good headline because it doesn't evoke or interest potential guests. On the other hand, a headline like "A minimally aesthetic villa with good ambiance and close to the airport" can evoke interest from potential guests who are looking for something like this while browsing listings.

How to Draft a Top-Notch Headline

The following are some of the tips that can help you to get more views for your listing:

- Understand that there is a 50-character limit for headlines while creating a listing. Write only what is important and what needs to be said to gain interest. Don't just stuff generic keywords that are clearly only there to increase search engine ranking.
- Use abbreviations whenever needed to reduce the characters that are being used. For example, "BR" is used for bedroom and "APT" is used for apartment.
- Use descriptive words whenever crafting headlines, as guests feel more connected with their usage.
- Highlight the amenities that you think the guests will love.

The Formula for a Great Headline

Writing a great headline is an art and should be learned by hosts if they are writing their headlines themselves.

We will provide you with the three popular formulas that hosts can use to write great headlines without hiring a copywriter.

Formula 1:

Adjective + Type of property + with + Amenities that are being provided

Example:

"Vast Apartment with a pool and a spacious bed"

Formula 2:

Adjective + Type of property + Proximity from nearest destination + with + Amenities that are being provided

Example:

"Spacious villa 20 mins drive from Downtown with a private pool, snooker, and a kitchen"

Formula 3:

Adjective + Type of property + great for + Experience that you are providing for the guests

Example:

"Private Outdoor cottage, great for romantic getaways"

Be creative and innovative with the formulas provided above to gain maximum interest from guests while they are browsing through listings.

Five Fields You Need to Fill While Creating a Listing on Airbnb

When providing information about your listing on the Airbnb website, you will need to ensure that the following fields are filled in correctly.

- **Aircover**

You need to accept the field that says that the listing is protected with Aircover. Aircover offers comprehensive coverage for all bookings. It covers guests for issues related to common problems such as cancellations by hosts, listing inaccuracies, and other issues like difficulties checking in.

Aircover also has a 24-hour safety hotline for both hosts and guests. Aircover can also help guests to gain access to specially trained security agents if something unfortunate happens at the listing.

- **About This Space**

This is the field where you need to enter all your main description details. Information about your listing should be provided here, highlighting all the reasons why your guests will love their stay. Refer to the sections on description writing to learn what to enter in this field.

- **Where You'll Sleep**

As guests are often specific about beds, you need to provide the number of beds and mattresses you are offering for the guests in this field.

- **What This Place Offers**

In this field, you need to enter all the amenities that you will provide for your guests. Ensure that you don't miss any amenities.

- **House Rules**

In this field, you need to enter all the rules that you will enforce while your guests are there. Emphasize that they need to follow all these rules and explain what the consequences are for breaking them.

Writing a Great Description

The description is what will let the guests know about all the important information regarding the property. If someone was hooked by your headline and cover photo, then they will be reading your description to understand what experience you are trying to provide for them. Writing descriptions can be a tough task, especially if you are not a very good writer.

Your writing shouldn't just provide information about your listing but should also evoke the guest's imagination and excitement about booking your property. A good description is hard to create, but with the guide provided below, you can easily create a charming description for your Airbnb listing.

What Should I Include?

When reading a description, guests should learn the following information without any difficulty:

- Guests need to be aware of all the sleeping arrangements that are available for them. Guests need to know the number of beds available and their size from the description.
- Guests need to learn about all the important and outstanding amenities that are available on the property from the description.
- If you are offering just a part of the property, then you need to mention which rooms will be available for the guests to stay in.
- In the description, you need to provide information about the neighborhood and whether there are any tourist attractions nearby.

How Do I Organize My Description?

It is so easy to deviate from an organized structure while writing a description, as there are no strict rules provided by Airbnb. Maintaining a good structure is important for guests to be able to read your description thoroughly.

- Organize the description into sections and subsections with the help of headings and subheadings. You need to have several dedicated sections such as "Amenities," "Rooms" available, and "Beds" according to what your property provides.
- Always use bulleted lists whenever you are listing items. For example, while listing the amenities provided, use the bulleted lists to make them more visually appealing and easier to read and remember.
- Don't hesitate, as a host, to include information that has already been mentioned. If it is important, then there is nothing wrong with mentioning it twice.
- Don't use filler words or write sentences like "We provide the best dishwasher in the area." These filler sentences can be cliché and can discourage guests from actually booking the listing.
- Instead of providing a little information about everything, provide complete information about whatever you consider most important.

How Do I Craft a Helpful Description?

The main goal of a description is to encourage guests to book your listing and give you the opportunity to host them. To motivate them to book your listing, you need to provide as much information as possible. For example, info such as the

Wi-Fi speed that you provide can be valuable information that guests will want to know.

Information in your description should include the following:

- Does the listing have a hair dryer?
- Does the listing have kitchen appliances?
- Does the listing provide cold and hot water?
- What are the nearest attractions to the listing?
- Is there a good coffee maker available?
- If it is an apartment, is an elevator available?
- Is their parking space available?
- How close is the airport or public transportation from the listing?
- Is there a gym available on site?

You might also include location or event-specific questions and answers if you receive a lot of tourists in your area during the holiday season or because of events, such as Comic Con.

Additional questions in your description might include the following:

- How far is Niagara Falls from the location?
- Are there any local travel guides available nearer to the location?
- How far is the listing from the Comic Con event?
- Can I get costumes near the listing for the Comic Con event?

Example of a Good Description:

This unique property combines all the best that Paris has to offer, the combination of arts, fashion, and love. With top-end amenities like a hot tub, neon lights, and ambient rooms, along with a breathtaking city view, this is a perfect getaway for everyone.

It's in a great location with quick access to all the popular city destinations and to several malls, pubs, the airport, and convenience stores.

This is a good description because we have provided all the top amenities, what we are offering, and information about the area in just a few words.

Example of a Bad Description:

A good place to stay with your friends and family. You can visit this place to find happiness and get away from your problems. All the amenities are wonderful and will make your stay perfect. All popular locations are easily accessible.

This might be considered a bad description because the flow is generic and we haven't provided details about any top amenities or what we have to offer to guests in the description.

If you are still not comfortable about writing a description on your own, then you can hire someone with good writing skills to do it for you. You can easily hire freelancers from websites such as Fiverr or Upwork to do this job for you.

Images for Listings

Images are the most important component in your listing because they are what will most attract a guest's attention while searching for places to stay on the Airbnb app or website. Outstanding photos that you have uploaded for your property can trigger the response action of a potential guest.

Boring and cliché photos can make it difficult for you to win bookings over your competitors in your area. You need to think like a professional when uploading photos for your listing. Uploading average photos that were taken with your smartphone may decrease the overall potential of your property and hurt the likelihood of getting bookings.

Why are photos important?

While descriptions are great and can present a big picture of what you are offering to guests, it's hard to convince people unless they can see it for themselves. Guests primarily depend on photographs, pricing, and reviews to decide whether or not a property might be a suitable choice for them.

Your photographs help them judge your property, the aesthetics, and the overall space according to their requirements. Only after going through these images will they read reviews or descriptions of the amenities you will provide.

How do I test the performance of my photos?

Different kinds of photographs possess different attractive characteristics. It is important to constantly check on the performance of your cover photo. As the cover photo is the first impression for your guests, you need to make sure it is up to date so that visitors will not be disappointed if you've made changes to the property and haven't updated your cover photo.

You can check the stats regarding clicks on your listing from your Airbnb account. Keep your cover photo fresh and check whether these changes increase or decrease the number of clicks on your listing to eliminate any bad photos that you may have used.

What is a Good Cover Photo?

A good cover photo should have all the following qualities:

- It should be unique.
- It should show off the home's best features.
- Everything in the cover photo should be clean and orderly.
- It should look professional.
- It should create an emotional connection with the property.

After the testing phase, you can use the best-performing cover photo as your permanent cover photo for your listing. Better photos usually have a ripple effect associated with them. The more clicks you get, the more bookings will be coming in, and therefore your profits will increase, too.

Hire a Professional Photographer

If you are serious about your Airbnb business, we recommend you hire a professional photographer instead of taking the photos by yourself.

A professional photographer is a better choice for getting more clicks on your listing for the following reasons:

- Professionals have mastery over their art, and therefore they can take images using different modes to capture the right style for your property. Professional photographers also use both artificial and natural lighting to ensure that the photographs are engaging and attractive.
- Professional photographers will be able to differentiate between a good photo and a great photo.

As individuals, we are usually satisfied with the good photos that most other Airbnb hosts upload. Professionals, on the other hand, will strive to take great photos that will immediately grab guests' attention.

- Professionals usually have more knowledge about the Airbnb guest demographics and can take photos that guests care about. Hiring someone with experience in Airbnb photography is essential. Search online on sites such as freelancer.com, or contact your local professionals to get started with getting great photos for your listing.

How to Stage Your Space for Taking Photos

You need to remember the following tips before staging your images with a photographer:

- Ensure that the space is clean and orderly. Complete the cleaning before staging any photos.
- Ensure that everything in the space looks organized. All the chairs and rugs need to be properly aligned, and make sure that cables or cords are out of sight.
- If you are taking shower photos, make sure all the basic amenities are shown in the photos and the bathroom itself is clean.
- Ensure that the photographs are as aesthetically pleasing as possible. To be aesthetic, the photos' content needs to be minimal and not cluttered.
- When you are staging your images, make it feel like a home instead of a regular hotel room. Airbnb is an industry that provides an experience that is different from regular hotels, and you need to display these

details in your images. They should evoke a home-like feeling for potential guests.

Get All the Shots

When you are choosing photos for your listing, ensure that you have included different detailed views and close-up shots so that visitors have all the information about the different amenities present on your property.

Here are some tips:

- Ensure that you have all kinds of shots, including close-up shots, top angle shots, and shots that emphasize different highlights of your listing.
- Show a perfect view so that guests can envision themselves staying at your property.
- When taking pictures, try to provide answers to questions that guests usually have. Show them rooms that guests usually care about, including the kitchen, bathroom, and bedrooms.

Make Your Photos Great Photos

When you hire a professional photographer, it is your responsibility to get the most out of them. Use the following tips to ensure that your photos are of high quality and will impress your potential guests:

- Ensure that the lighting for your photographs is great. Use natural lighting whenever possible to ensure that there is good crispiness and ambiance in the photographs. While night photographs can be a good option to reflect how your property looks at

night, they cannot help you create a good ambiance for your property without proper lighting. You need to use artificial equipment to create good lighting for your night photographs on your listing.
- Ensure that the photographer is composing the photographs well.
- You also need to mention to your photographer that the images shouldn't be overexposed or underexposed.

Once you have images in hand from the photographer, choose the best wide-angle shot from the bunch and select it as your cover photo. It is always hard to predict which image will perform better. Test out a few images before choosing one as your permanent cover photo and see how your conversion rate changes.

Baseline Pricing

The success of your listing will mostly depend on the baseline pricing that you have set up. Baseline pricing refers to the hourly/nightly price you will be posting to your listing, excluding cleaning and other additional fees. When you are setting up baseline pricing, you need to understand the competition and what they are charging. Analyze the demographics and focus on maintaining a price that is competitive and that your potential guests can pay.

You can also adjust your prices according to demand and season. For example, you could set a lower price during weekdays and a higher price during the weekends.

What strategy should I use?

Hosts usually use three strategies when setting their nightly rates. You might choose one of these strategies depending on how aggressive or conservative your business approach is.

- **Charge less than the current market.**

With this strategy, more bookings will be ensured, but your profit potential will be decreased. If you are okay with lower profits for a while, especially during the initial days, in exchange for getting more reviews, then this is a great strategy.

- **Charge the same as the current market but provide more amenities.**

With this strategy, you will be charging the same nightly rates as the current market but will also be providing additional amenities that other listings are not providing. While the initial investment is high, this strategy will assure more bookings.

- **Provide better amenities and charge a premium.**

With this strategy, you will be targeting premium customers in the market. You need to provide something unique when you are charging a premium for your nightly rates. However, with this strategy, even with fewer bookings per month, you can earn high profits.

Pricing Strategies

As an Airbnb host, apart from baseline pricing, you will be charging several other fees according to how many guests are staying at your property and how many days they are going to be there.

Setting these additional fees can be a tricky task, as you need to be reasonable while also trying to increase your profit potential. Lots of beginners in the Airbnb business set these prices too high, which results in interested guests deciding against staying at their property, even if they provide better amenities and the property itself is what they had in mind.

This section will help you understand how to set these fees with a well-thought-out strategy so that you can increase your profit potential while ensuring that your guests will be happy with the service you are providing.

Cleaning Fee

The cleaning fee is one of the most commonly charged fees for listings on Airbnb. These charges start from as little as $10 for small listings and go up to hundreds of dollars for bigger listings such as villas.

It is recommended that you charge below the average rate of your competitors to have an advantage, especially if there is a lot of competition in your locality for property listings. Once you get more consistent bookings, you can slowly increase cleaning fees to cover your expenses.

As a rule, if you are in the beginning stages where you need a greater number of visitors to your listing so that your business can get started with positive reviews, you should charge less than what your competition is charging for a cleaning fee.

Bold Strategy: Charge Nothing

If you want to increase your number of bookings during a dull season, or when you are desperate for initial bookings of your listing, you could opt to charge nothing for a cleaning fee.

While you may be lowering your profits for a while, you can reduce these costs by following these tips:

- If your listing is small, you can quickly clean the listing by yourself and turn over the property before the next guest arrives.
- If there is no other way than hiring a pro for cleaning your property, you can raise the nightly rate slightly. If the guest stays for only a few days, you will be cutting down on some of your profits with this strategy. You can, however, keep your profits if guests book your listing for more days.

Common Strategy: Charge Less Than Your Competition

If you want to have a competitive advantage over other popular listings in your area, then we suggest you charge a little bit less than the rates that they are charging. Adjust the cleaning rates according to the bookings you receive. As an example, if you have 10 separate bookings and your profit margin has decreased a little, you can increase the cleaning fee for the next 10 bookings.

Security Deposit

The security deposit is usually collected by all Airbnb hosts to ensure that if any damage happens, they can claim the amount to receive compensation for the damages. A security deposit is usually charged by Airbnb to the guests' credit cards.

While a security deposit ensures that hosts have the utmost protection from bad guests, it can also reduce your bookings, especially if you charge a high security deposit.

According to many hosts, the security deposit should usually not be less than $200 and not over $1,000, even for luxurious properties. As you can always file a claim for Airbnb host protection covered under the $1 million plan, you should only allot these fees for common damages that occasionally happen.

Additional Guest Fees

Every property allows a maximum number of guests, and this information is usually provided in the description. If the number of guests increases, then an additional guest fee needs to be charged. Usually, $15 is charged, and this can extend up to $100 depending on the property.

Service Fee

A service fee is charged by Airbnb whenever a booking happens. You will not receive any part of the service fee when a booking is made. Depending on the locality and demand for listings in your area, as well as the season, service fees will vary.

Turn on Instant Book

The instant book feature is a great tool that hosts can utilize to improve their booking rate. If you are a beginner trying to get your first few bookings, then "switching on" this option can immediately book your property with the guest without you having to verify and accept their request.

Switching on the instant book option not only increases your booking rate but also improves your SEO ranking, so more potential guests will be seeing your listing in the top results. Search Engine Optimization (SEO) refers to how Airbnb's default search engine ranks listings in your area.

Many superhosts do not switch on this option, however, because there are a lot of cancellations that take place when guests don't have anything to lose. You also will be given less control of who will be staying on your property, making it less secure than the normal Airbnb booking process.

How do I use the instant book feature to my advantage?

It is a known fact that any great tool has certain downsides. To counter the cons that come with the instant book option, here are a few things you can do to eliminate the disadvantages from a business perspective:

- Block some dates off when you know that people will be coming to stay on the property. Airbnb provides dates that you can open instant book for in advance, making it easy for you to manage your calendar and avoid dealing with the hassle of last-minute bookings.
- Instead of cleaning the room before a new check-in, clean the room after a guest checks out. This will make it easy to manage any guests who book your property on short notice using the instant book option.
- It is also possible to cancel instant book reservations right from your app or on the website. If you find that certain guests may not be good for your

property, then by all means you can message them and say that their reservation has been canceled.

Marketing Your Listing on Other Platforms

While most potential guests search and book listings from the Airbnb app or website, as a host, you need to market your listing on different platforms to ensure that you get the most out of your business. Especially if you are a beginner getting your first few bookings, this part can be tough. During this time, you can depend on some of the marketing strategies mentioned below.

- **Marketing With Email Addresses**

One of the better ways to ensure that your listing is always booked is to send emails to guests who have already visited your property. Many guests like to revisit places they liked, so when they're looking for a place to go for vacation or an event, those good experiences will come to mind first.

While there is no way to predict when a guest will want to visit again, sending emails to them is considered a good way of letting them know that your property is available. If they are recurring customers, you can offer a discount to them specifically.

To collect email addresses, you can ask guests for the information either during the check-in or check-out process. Offer a free breakfast or provide a complimentary drink to whoever provides their email address to you. Don't ask them further if they say no the first time and are not willing to give that information to you.

Once you collect enough emails, you can register with a service such as Mailchimp to send emails to everyone on the list once a month. Don't send too many emails because that can lead to people unsubscribing from them.

- **Create Your Own Website**

You can create a brand new website for your listing to collect leads using email and phone numbers. In the digital guide you have provided, you can include a link to the website URL. Make the URL stand out by using bold letters and a red font.

To make the website interesting, provide information about the nearby tourist locations or coffee shops so that the website doesn't feel like just advertising to collect email addresses from guests.

- **Social Media**

Social media is where most people are spending hours on their smartphones these days. You can use the exposure that social media platforms provide to promote your listings.

Post all the photographs that you have taken for your listing on Instagram. As Instagram is a visually rich social media app, you need to ensure that your photos are high quality. You can also use TikTok to provide some quick tips for guests who are visiting your property.

You might also use Facebook to target your potential guests. Facebook provides a paid advertising opportunity for hosts where they can target a set of demographics. With good research, you can narrow down the audience that will be interested in your listing and target them specifically with alluring photos or by offering steep discounts.

- **Google AdWords**

Google AdWords allows businesses to reach potential customers easily through its search engine. The majority of Airbnb users will use a search engine first before opening the Airbnb website when searching for properties to stay in a specific area. It is possible to use Google AdWords to target a specific search query, such as "Properties to stay for 2 days near New York downtown," and offer your Airbnb property as an advertisement. The aim is for potential guests to be interested in your link and click the advertisement to book your listing. For Google advertising, you must pay according to the number of clicks your advertisement has received. To be precise, Google AdWords is a paid marketing strategy that hosts can use to attract potential guests.

It is true that Google AdWords costs more than $1 per click, but the clicks also have a high conversion rate, which turns into consistent bookings, thereby directly increasing your profits.

Airbnb SEO

Close to 80% of the bookings on Airbnb happen because of specific search results. When someone searches a keyword, your listing needs to be in the top results for you to secure consistent bookings throughout the year. Not many users of Airbnb will be patient enough to scroll through more than 10 pages to discover your listing and add it as their perfect staying option.

SEO increases your visibility in the Airbnb search engine and will directly influence the number of bookings that you get. Hosts use Airbnb SEO to improve their search engine rankings for different keywords and to dominate their local SEO algorithm.

SEO does not just refer to the use of keywords; it's about optimizing your listing focused on popular keywords so that it will show up near the top of search results every time. Simply adding a keyword to your heading or description won't make you a top result. You need to adhere to relevant criteria that will make the SEO algorithm believe that your listing is what people are looking for.

There are more than 100 factors that Airbnb algorithms analyze while ranking their listings. While reviews are important to rank higher, there are several other factors as mentioned below that can push your listing into the top results for the popular keywords in your locality or city.

Fast Response Times

One of the primary factors that affect your SEO ranking is your response times for queries asked by visitors on the site. When your response time is quicker than your competition, then the algorithm will understand that there is a higher chance for guests to leave you positive reviews.

You can use automated messaging tools or hire a virtual assistant to always maintain a history of good response time.

Listing Age

While this is not a major factor of your Airbnb business, it can still help your listing rank higher than the other listings. All the new listings are given a little more preference than the older listings, as Airbnb believes that new listings need a little bit of a push due to not having many reviews yet.

However, once you have three to five bookings, your listing will then have to start competing with all the other older, established listings. While you might think about resetting your listing and starting anew in order to take advantage of this, it is important to remember that all of your reviews will be erased when you reset a listing. It is not possible to use this algorithm to your advantage if your listing is older with lots of good reviews.

Booking Rate Percentage

Booking rate refers to the number of bookings that have happened vs the number of people who have visited your listing when they searched for properties to stay in.

For example, if 50 people have visited your listing and only 5 people booked with you, then the booking rate percentage is 10%. The algorithm will favor listings with a higher booking rate percentage.

Improve your booking rate percentage by following the tips below:

- Ensure that the listing is of high quality.
- Add a great cover photo.
- Ensure that the price is set according to your potential guest demographics.

Pricing

In the short-term rental business, pricing always plays a major role in determining whether or not your listings should be displayed at the top. When the price is lower, more guests will be keen to book your property. While this may decrease your profits a bit, if you want to improve your Airbnb SEO ranking, then we suggest you adjust your pricing in a way that is competitive to get those initial bookings.

Listings Should Be Complete

For the Airbnb SEO algorithm to favor your listing, you need to ensure that all the sections within the listing are filled in properly. You can provide bulleted lists and checkboxes to make sure that the listing looks as professional as possible.

Chapter 5

How to Run Your Airbnb Property

Once guests book your property for a stay, you will receive a notification from Airbnb saying that a guest is arriving on the specified date. The guest will also be informed by Airbnb's automated messaging system that their booking has been confirmed for a particular date. From the moment this message is sent until they check out, it is your responsibility to provide them with a great experience that they will be happy about. This chapter focuses on helping you understand several useful tips and common practices that are used by successful hosts to provide a superhost experience for their guests.

Ensuring a Smooth Check-In

Your initial task is to inform your guests about the check-in process. Not everyone has visited an Airbnb listing before, and so you need to provide clear instructions about when they can check into the property every time.

Use a simple message format as shown below and ensure that your communication is as casual as possible.

- Say “Hi” and express your sincere gratitude for booking your listing in two simple sentences.
- Send them the check-in instructions, including such details as how to unlock the door and what to expect from their stay.
- Send them a list of frequently asked questions (FAQ) that covers concerns guests usually have. Invite your guests to ask if they have additional questions about anything. Be sure to respond promptly and don’t leave them hanging.

Questions might include the following:

- From which direction should we approach your house?
- What amenities are available?
- What are the nearest tourist locations to your property?
- What instructions should we follow while parking our cars?
- How do we log in to your Wi-Fi?

Follow-up Message

You should send a follow-up message a day before your guests’ check-in date. A lot of guests don’t check their messages immediately after they book, so you need to make sure they receive the information they need. Even if they’ve seen your initial messages, it never hurts to offer reminders and reinforce important information. In the second message that you send, you need to provide several pieces of information as shown below to ensure that guests don't miss anything important.

- Reconfirm the booking details.
- Mention and emphasize the check-in time.
- Provide the relevant directions to your property. You can also provide coordinates to offer a precise location, especially if it is very rural.
- Mention the parking instructions again.
- Give them the Wi-Fi details.
- Provide your contact information.

Preparing for Guest Check-In

It is your responsibility to be absolutely ready for your guests to arrive. This section provides some of the important information that can help you prepare in advance for a good first impression.

- You need to make sure that the listing is accurate and portrays what your property is actually like. Guests are often disappointed when they see something that is not equal to what they expected when they booked their stay. It is for this reason that we stress investing in a professional photographer to provide attractive and accurate images for your listing.
- Ensure that a small welcome gift is provided for your guests, along with a house guide that will help them navigate all the important information related to your property. Be sure to also add directions to let them know where they need to look first. For example, if your listing is located near a coffee shop, then give

directions to the coffee shop if it will be easier for them to first locate this landmark, then move on to your property.

- Make sure that all the cleaning is done according to the checklists we've provided in the next chapter.
- Make sure that the Wi-Fi is available for the guests even before they check in, as not all of them will have cell coverage, especially if they are international travelers.
- Check for any bad odors that may impact guests' impression of your listing. Make sure to find out the reason for these bad odors and try to clear it out through extensive cleaning.
- Stock all essential supplies.

Welcoming Guests

When welcoming and handling the check-in process, you can do it either in-person or from a remote location. We will provide information about both of these ways to make sure that you don't miss any important steps.

In-Person Check-Ins

To be fair, in-person check-ins are becoming rarer and rarer due to the development and usage of efficient smart locks.

However, there are some cases where in-person check-ins might be the best way to go:

- If your properties are large and you are hosting a large number of people, a guided tour during the check-in process can help your guests get comfortable and feel at home.

- If it is complicated to access your listing using the directions, then in-person check-ins are recommended. For example, if your listing is in a remote location, then this is a recommended way to welcome your guests.
- If you have complicated amenities and want to give the guests a guided tour, then an in-person check-in is recommended.
- If you receive senior citizens who are usually first-time Airbnb visitors, then in-person check-ins are recommended.

In this check-in process, you need to receive the guests first and welcome them with a small gift. Once they are ready, offer them a quick tour of the property and give them the keys. If there is a smart lock, then give them the code.

Invite them to text or call whenever there is a need. Answer any queries that the guests have before leaving the property.

Remote Self-Check-In

Doing a remote self-check-in is easy and the most preferred way for hosts to use these days due to the pandemic situation. Before the pandemic, a lot of check-ins were in-person check-ins, but with the introduction of social distancing rules, the Airbnb business has moved toward the self-check-in process. It is expected that many hosts will continue with this check-in process either permanently or for at least a few more years, as it is so convenient.

Why is it so convenient?

- It is flexible and provides security at the same time.

- It can help you manage your time for other more pressing tasks.
- It can help you to manage your property even from other parts of the world.

You should have already sent your guests instructions about how to check in to the property. Give them the pin for the locks to open the main door. We will be discussing in detail how to automate the check-in process in the next chapter.

Communication During Guest Stays

To receive five-star reviews from guests, you need to be available for them should they have any questions while on your property. While you can hire virtual assistants or use tools such as Airdna to copy templates and quickly send messages, you still need to be available and able to communicate effectively with guests if you want to give them a five-star experience as a host.

- **Take Their Problems Personally**

Whenever you receive a query or request for help from your guests, most of the time these queries will be basic and not very complex. So, whenever you are replying to them with instructions, do so casually and make the texts feel like you are helping a friend or a family member.

- **Create a Sense of Urgency**

When you are communicating, make sure you convey the fact that you are addressing the problem with a sense of urgency. Instead of saying, "I will call the plumber soon," say, "I will send the plumber immediately."

- **Redirect Them to the Guest Guide**

Most of the answers to queries about amenities will already be provided in the guest guide. You need to nudge them toward the page where the instructions are outlined for them.

- **Answer Guests' Questions Quickly**

There is nothing more important than replying to messages immediately regarding guests' issues. If necessary to keep up with a busy hosting business or multiple properties, hire a virtual assistant or a property management company to manage these messages for you.

Dealing with Issues During Guest Stays

While hosting guests, sometimes problems may arise where you need to settle the issue and ensure that the guest has no further problems. While unfortunate, it is quite common for hosts to make mistakes.

As a host, you need to be quick to solve these issues. Take a look at some of the tips we have provided about what to do in these situations.

1. First of all, apologize.

Even though maintenance issues are common, you should be courteous and apologize to your guests for these inconveniences during their stay. Offer them a small gift or refund part of their nightly rate as recompense for these issues.

2. Fix the problem as soon as possible.

When a guest has raised an issue, immediately try to solve the issue without delay. If you are not near the property, then you need to call your management company so that they can send a professional as soon as possible. If you are not dependent on a management company, then it is important to have an established relationship with professionals nearby who can respond quickly and fix any issues.

Sometimes guests may also cause problems for you by not following the rules or making too much noise. During these times, you need to first message them politely, and if they are not obliging, then you may have to contact Airbnb's customer service.

Ensuring a Smooth Check-Out

Your guests must check out of the property once their stay has ended. It is important to provide the same level of efficiency that you provided during the check-in process.

Follow some of the strategies listed below to ensure that your guests have a smooth check-out experience:

- **Be Accurate Regarding Check-Out Time**

You need to state the check-out time specifically to the guests. Many people tend to estimate the check-out time and do not double-check their Airbnb booking. It is important to stress the time so that your next guests will not have any issues during their check-in process.

- **Provide Instructions**

If you are managing your listing remotely, then you may have to provide clear check-out instructions for your guests when they are leaving the property. Include how to lock the doors with the help of a smart lock or return keys. If cleaning personnel have already arrived, then they can lock the property instead of the guests after turnover is completed.

- **Provide a Small Parting Gift**

Providing a parting gift can help your guests leave with a good impression. These gifts don't need to be anything fancy but should represent sincerity for hosting them. A box of chocolates, fresh flowers from the garden, or a $20 Amazon gift card are a few common parting gifts provided by hosts for their guests.

- **Send Friendly Messages**

While guests are staying on the property, send them brief, friendly messages, such as asking them to try the custom coffee powder you have provided for their stay if they want to. Remember to send a parting message to say "thank you."

Chapter 6

Cleaning Guide for Hosts

One of the major aspects of maintaining your Airbnb business is cleaning and setting up the property before guests check in. Many new hosts spend most of their time setting prices and marketing their properties to get more bookings, but they forget how important it is to ensure that their guests are receiving a first-class experience by keeping the property well maintained and clean. As a host, it is important for you to prepare your property in a way that meets guests' expectations. If their first impression is bad, then you may get negative reviews, which will have a ripple effect and reduce future bookings, as well as your profits from your Airbnb hosting business.

In fact, cleaning and resetting the property is one of the more challenging tasks involved in the Airbnb business. This chapter focuses on providing information about how to clean and reset your space for each new guest that comes and stays on your property.

Maintaining Your Space

Before diving deep into the cleaning aspects of managing your property, let us look in detail at some specific aspects you should prioritize in your space to have long-term success in the Airbnb business. All hosts are expected to maintain their property to ensure that guests have a positive, safe stay.

1. Smoke and Carbon Monoxide Detectors

Safety should be the top priority in any business. Even if you have property damage and liability insurance for your property, it is important to ensure that your guests will be alerted during unfortunate situations such as a fire. It is important to have smoke and carbon monoxide detectors throughout the property so that your guests feel secure. You also need to regularly check and verify that they are working as they are supposed to.

Make sure that the batteries aren't dead in these detectors. Apart from these detectors, you also need to place fire extinguishers around your property. The number of fire extinguishers you need to place should be compliant with your jurisdiction requirements.

2. Doors and Windows

Maintaining doors and windows is usually an easy task, but sometimes carelessness can cause potential issues for guests. Before every check-in, ensure that all doors and windows are in working order. Your main checks should be whether or not the locks are working properly for all the doors on your property.

All windows should also be closed properly without any drafts coming in. If any windows or doors are too difficult to open and close, they should be immediately checked by a professional. Doors and windows that don't close well can be a potential safety hazard, especially if pets and children are present.

3. Heating, Ventilation, and Air Conditioning (HVAC)

Maintaining and controlling the temperature of your space is one of the more important considerations that you want to provide for your guests. As guests are usually from different parts of the world, they may be comfortable with different temperatures. Not having good heating, ventilation, or air conditioning can result in guests ending their stay abruptly if they are too uncomfortable. You need to thoroughly check these appliances and also ensure that there are no electric malfunctions.

If there is any problem with HVAC during your guests' stay, then be sure to make getting this repaired your top priority. Apologize to guests for the inconvenience caused and offer them a small gift as compensation. You might even extend their stay for a day as a peace offering.

If the HVAC is going to take a long time to repair, then you may need to book them a nearby hotel room while they wait. While this is an extreme scenario, it is your responsibility to take care of your guests in all adverse situations, especially if they've traveled far and have nowhere else to go.

4. Water Heater

You also need to check that the water heater is working perfectly. You need to make sure that both cold and hot water options are available for your guests.

What Other Aspects Should I be Monitoring?

1. Check for any water leaks. Ensure that they are immediately taken care of.
2. Clear away any excess leaves on your property. While extra leaves or foliage is not a major problem, they can give a bad first impression.
3. Make sure that there is insect repellant and that measures have been taken to deter rodents from your property.
4. You also need to constantly check for bed bugs, especially during the winter months. During the summer, get your property treated by pest control to make sure there is no sign of ants.
5. There should be trash bags in every room so that your guests will be motivated to clean up after themselves instead of throwing trash on the floor.

Cleaning Your Space

Cleaning your space after guests have checked out is one of the major headaches involved with the Airbnb business. As guests pay a separate charge just for cleaning the space, don't expect the place to be spotless after they leave. This is considered a major headache by hosts because you need to be physically present to clean the property if you are not able to pay for professional cleaners. It is also the task that will take the most time compared to other hosting responsibilities.

The larger the property, the more time it will take to clean everything, and this can increase exponentially. Even though cleaning is time-consuming, it is important to do it right if you want to get those positive reviews. Each guest that comes to your property will expect the listing to be clean and look like new for their stay.

Irrespective of whether you will be doing the cleaning yourself or hiring a pro, you need to be aware of the following information.

The Turnover Process

There is a difference between cleaning your home and the cleaning you need to do for your Airbnb listing. When guests enter your property, they need to experience a similar impression usually associated with nice hotels. The best way to evoke these emotions is by doing the turnover cleaning properly.

Let's discuss step-by-step the processes that need to be followed for turnover cleaning and resetting.

1. Check for Damages

Before starting with the actual cleaning, it is important to check for damages that may have been incurred on your property. It is a commonly known fact that people can be hard on things that they don't own, and so it is very normal to see a few things out of place or even damaged each time guests check out.

Again, the best way to prepare for this situation is to have a security deposit in place to be sure guests can compensate you for the damages that they are responsible for. It is also important to accurately document the damages so that you don't accidentally charge the wrong guests for the damage caused. Stains on bed sheets are the most common damages that Airbnb hosts usually deal with. Instead of just washing them, replace them with new ones.

2. Restock Essentials

For every stay, you need to restock essentials such as toilet paper and soap. It is also important to stock the property with backups of these items so that your guests will not run out. While it is suggested to place items such as facial tissues and paper towels in racks, it is not a mandatory requirement. Stocking these additional items, however, can make a good impression and increase your chances of getting a positive review.

3. Reset Rooms

Once you or the professional cleaners complete the turnover process for each room, have someone do a walkthrough to ensure that they are as pleasant and presentable as possible. Imagine yourself as a guest and how it would feel if this was where you were staying for a few days for a premium fee.

Turnover Cleaning Checklists

Every host has their own approach to the turnover process. While we leave it to you to determine how best to do your cleaning, we do encourage you to use the following checklists to ensure the best possible guest experience.

Tip:

Whenever you enter a room for cleaning, first ensure that all the towels and linens are taken to the laundry. Also, while you are cleaning the rooms, load and start the dishwasher.

Checklist for Kitchen

The kitchen will usually be the messiest room on your property if guests have been cooking and have left the pans in the sink.

Use the following list to clean the kitchen:

1. First of all, when you enter the kitchen, spray the oven with a cleaner, as it may take some time to set before scrubbing.
2. Wipe down all the appliances as well as the cabinets and sink with a disinfectant. You can use a cloth to clean the countertops, then sweep and mop the floors.
3. After you've cleaned the appliances, scrub the oven. Usually, ovens need to be cleaned thoroughly at least once a month.
4. Clean all the dishes, pans, and utensils in the sink with a good cleaning detergent. If there is a dishwasher, then you can use it to complete the process quickly.
5. Spray the room with a good air freshener that is not too strong.

Checklist for Bathroom

The bathroom can sometimes be one of the toughest rooms to clean. Don't forget to wear a mask and gloves before entering to clean.

1. First of all, ensure that there are no traces of hair in the toilet, in the shower, or on the bathroom floor. Sometimes hair can get stuck and block the water flow.
2. Disinfect all surfaces with a good bathroom cleaner. You need to ensure that the sink, shower, and shower door are cleaned.
3. Scrub the toilet, including the bowl, cover, and exterior.
4. Clean the mirror perfectly. Check for any scratches.
5. Once everything is completed, clean the floor with a good mop.

Checklist for Bedrooms

Bedrooms need to be well taken care of, as guests spend most of their time in these rooms.

Clean these rooms following the steps below in order:

1. First of all, wipe down all the surfaces neatly.
2. Sweep the floor or vacuum carpet thoroughly. Ensure that there are no hairs or any trash that may have been left by the previous guests.
3. At the end, remake the bed with clean sheets. Arrange the pillows in a professional and presentable way.

In addition to these checklists, you also need to wipe down and disinfect all the surfaces in the common areas.

Organizing the Cleaning Process

Irrespective of whether you are doing the cleaning process by yourself or hiring a pro, you need to follow certain rules to ensure that the process is as smooth and efficient as possible.

- **Always Follow a Checklist**

Following a checklist is the easiest way to make sure that you are not skipping or forgetting any tasks that need to be done. When we follow a checklist, we streamline the process so things get done quickly as we work toward fixed goals. If you don't enjoy cleaning, then checking those boxes off a checklist makes it a bit easier to get through so you will ensure that your guests have the best experience possible on the property.

- **Prepare for Hiccups**

During any process, you will have hiccups from time to time, especially with tasks such as cleaning the property. If you find plumbing issues or electrical shortage issues while cleaning, immediately inform your professional connections to fix the problem promptly for you.

- **Stay Stocked Always**

As a host, it is important for you to have sufficient stock to immediately replace the basic essentials, towels, and linens that are required. You need to have at least two dozen towels and a ton of toilet paper to immediately replace them if guests need them.

Professional Cleaners

Not everyone has the time or desire to clean their property by themselves. If you are someone who feels stressed about cleaning, then hiring a professional cleaner will be a better option for you. Hiring a professional gives you confidence, as your listing will always look perfect for each new guest. This will surely increase the number of positive reviews you receive.

Hiring and outsourcing to cleaners also provides freedom and flexibility so you can focus on other tasks related to running your business, such as setting prices, communicating with the guests, or marketing.

What do I need to know about hiring professional cleaners?

1. Know what type of cleaner you need for your property. Professional cleaners can be costly, so you need someone who can do the work for you in less than an hour if your listing is small or of medium size. If your listing is large, then you need to hire someone who can work long hours or a group of cleaners who can do the work for you in the shortest amount of time.
2. Just like hiring for any other job, you need to first interview the cleaner and ensure that they are highly skilled and can handle the job like a pro. Cleaning professionally is a skill that requires efficiency and attention to detail.
3. Train the cleaners yourself and provide them with copies of the checklists you have created to ensure that they are following the instructions and not just cleaning what they want to.

4. Create your own system for judging the performance of the cleaner. You can also hire someone for quality control.

Note:

Sometimes cleaners will be unavailable due to personal or professional reasons. You need to ensure that you have backup cleaners who can do the job for you on short notice if someone is unavailable. Not having backup cleaners can be a bad idea, as guests will not be happy staying in rooms that are unclean and out of order.

Cleaning Company Suggestion:

Airbnb rental cleaning is usually outsourced to cleaning companies in the area. If you are not happy with your local services, then you can try out some of the professional cleaning companies such as TurnoverBnB and Merry Maids. Though both of these companies charge a premium, their services are the best you can find, and they will make the turnover process a lot easier for you as a host.

Chapter 7

Automating Your Business

Airbnb hosting is a great passive income opportunity that has helped individuals around the world gain financial freedom. This lucrative business opportunity is available to most people, even if they are nowhere near the property they will be listing. Your goal should be to understand the systems that are provided to you and use them to run the business passively. Almost everything in the Airbnb host business can be automated to boost your profits and let you follow your passions without worrying about the tedious work that is necessary to make your guests' experience great. With automation and outsourcing, you will still have absolute control over the process and can intervene whenever there is an issue.

This chapter focuses on providing information about the tools available to help you automate your business to save you a great deal of time. The primary essence of automation is to minimize the number of hours you have to spend managing the business while maximizing the dollars that you are earning.

Why is Automation Necessary?

One of the common reasons why hosts face failure on Airbnb is the burnout and frustration associated with it. Many hosts don't automate their business and instead try to manage all the work by themselves, which means they deal with stressful situations personally whenever there is an issue with guests or the property. Burnout can lead to a lapse in service quality, which leads to negative reviews and fewer bookings.

Instead of choosing profits as your main motive, you also need to focus on your sanity. Of course, it's important to keep your profits sustainable for your business. However, when you try to scale your business, you should be rational and accept that you will need the help of automation tools and a team of professionals to help manage your Airbnb business.

Setting Up Automation

Achieving automation for your Airbnb listings can be complicated, so follow our guide to make sure you set things up correctly.

A few things that a host should focus on first include the following:

- Figure out what you can handle and what you cannot. Doing things that you love about the Airbnb business and outsourcing anything that you are not keen on doing is a good strategy.
- Learn the art of negotiation to save on spending while outsourcing work.

We will now look at several automation workflows that can maximize the potential of your Airbnb business.

Automate Your Airbnb Guest Communication

Guest communication is a very important and time-consuming task that all guests expect from their hosts. All property managers need to provide this experience for guests so that they feel safe and not underwhelmed by their stay.

As a host, it is suggested that you message guests before, during, and after their stay. This basic etiquette leaves a good impression with guests, especially if they are tourists who are unfamiliar with the area. It is also important to answer all queries asked by the guests because not doing so can result in being penalized by Airbnb, and you may lose your superhost status. Being a superhost will result in more clicks on your listing and can increase profits for your Airbnb business over time.

It is not, however, logical to expect to be constantly free to answer your guests' queries. It may be impossible for you alone to answer every query that comes in, but with strategic automation, it is possible to decrease the amount of time you spend communicating with your guests.

1. Use Email Templates

It is not necessary that you create a personalized message for every specific question asked by your guests. Most of these inquiries are usually generic, so it is possible to use prebuilt templates that are provided by Airbnb automation tools such as Host Tools. You can access this service from hosttools.com with a premium account. Once you are in the dashboard of the website, you can select the "Email Templates" section to quickly get a list of recommended templates according to your needs. To find a specific email template, you can quickly search from the same interface.

These automation tools will provide pre-written message templates for all stages of the booking process.

As a host, you can use these templates as they are or modify them in some cases. You can also create a new template from scratch that you can use in the future.

Example Template:

Welcome to the check-in process for your Airbnb listing on 29th July 2022 in New York near Brooklyn Towers. We are happy to host you. To check in, you will need to enter the last four digits of your phone number as a pin on the smart lock. Once the pin is entered, click enter and wait for the door to open. Enjoy your stay!

You can now just change the date whenever you need to send the email to the next guests.

2. Automate Check-Ins

Guest check-in can be one of the stressful issues that you have to deal with. In-person check-ins, however, are not mandatory anymore for Airbnb properties, as there is now a lot of new technology, such as smart locks, which can make the check-in process seamless for you.

How does a smart lock work?

A smart lock is customizable and operates remotely so that the property is accessible for each of your guests. When hosts buy a smart lock, they are given a dedicated account on the smart lock servers to manage their property. Hosts can manage their accounts using a dedicated app.

Note: Different smart lock companies use different apps, so thoroughly read the guide that comes with your smart lock to download the correct app as a host and store the link to send it to guests after a booking is confirmed.

- Guests can use the mobile app provided by the brand of smart lock you use. You can send them the link to the app for a quick check-in process. Every popular smart lock comes with an app for hosts to quickly admit their guests using a unique code.
- These apps usually offer a dedicated account for the host. When a guest books the property, the app will automatically create a record in the host's account with the guest's name.
- When the booking is confirmed, the pin details will be sent to the smart lock servers. Hosts should now be able to send these details to the guests via chat or email so that guests can access the property when they arrive.

Smart locks come with a locking mechanism that will restrict access only after the check-in and not after the check-out. You also need to purchase a keypad to enter a pin manually if the guest doesn't have Wi-Fi or internet access to use the app.

This special code will be accessible for only a few hours and can be generated based on the guest's phone number or booking ID. It is not required that you visit the property to change keys, as this can be done remotely, making it a great option for many hosts who want to automate their Airbnb business.

In addition to the smart lock, it would be wise to add another layer of security by using an electronic lock on the front door. The difference between smart and electronic locks is that the code for smart locks will change according to the guests' details. Electronic locks, on the other hand, will keep the same code regardless of the guests. In order to check into their rooms using this kind of lock, guests will need to enter the main door code. The only problem here is that you need to set the code for the door while installing it on your property. It cannot be changed from a remote location. However, you can send this code to your guests easily, as they will need to first unlock the smart lock before being able to access the electronic lock that has a door code.

If you are tight on budget, you could also use a regular lockbox instead of electronic locks. These are mechanical, and so the guests need to be told how to unlock them. You can provide them with step-by-step instructions either via video or by using images so that there is no confusion about how to enter the property.

3. Automate Pricing

Setting good prices is important to ensure that guests are actually booking your listings. Lots of hosts, even with good amenities and excellent prebuilt listings, will not be able to get new bookings because they don't understand the pricing strategies that are necessary for their locality, depending on the season and events that are happening.

For example, if a festival is happening in your city, then you may need to increase your nightly rate to take advantage of the additional traffic, as there will be a larger demand for Airbnb listings during this time. There are several software options, such as Wheelhouse (use wheelhouse.com) that can handle the automation of your prices for you.

Software like this typically has a database of events and data related to different seasons to quickly customize the prices for your listings. You can set different parameters yourself to adjust how the software behaves. You can also set the maximum and minimum price points that the software can use to avoid reducing your profits because of the automatic dynamic price changes.

Outsourcing to Automate Different Tasks

To completely automate your Airbnb business, you need to spend more time outsourcing work to professionals to manage certain tasks involved in the business, such as communication, cleaning, and monitoring reviews. As most of these tasks are tedious and require a lot of time, it makes sense to hire virtual assistants from around the world using websites such as fiver.com or freelancer.com.

You should always, however, interview them before giving them the responsibility of handling your listings. Already having knowledge about the Airbnb business would be a good requirement for hiring a VA.

- **Outsource for Guest Communication**

New guests usually have questions. In fact, sometimes the questions are nonstop, especially during the check-in and check-out process or anytime they have a problem. If you want to automate this communication and respond appropriately and promptly, you can hire a virtual assistant who has experience specifically in handling Airbnb guests. Upwork is a good place to outsource for an hourly rate that fits your needs and the freelancer's experience level.

VAs hired this way may not be as perfect as software, so sometimes you may need to replace them with someone who performs better. There are several desktop and online tools that will help you monitor your contract employee's tasks and quality of work and customer service. Consider this data when deciding between a fixed-fee or hourly contract.

Spend a day or two brainstorming questions that guests may ask related to your locality and give the answers to your VA so that they don't have to rely on you again to answer these same questions.

- **Outsourcing for Guest Reviews**

All of the guests who stay on your property can review you as their host, and you as a host can review them as well once they have checked out from your listing. You can outsource the review process to a virtual assistant, as most of the time generic templates are used for guest reviewing and answering reviews written by guests for you.

VAs can review any reports provided by the cleaners once they look around for any damages. VAs should be efficient and professional when responding to all the reviews left by your guests to ensure that you leave a good impression as a host who cares about their guests' satisfaction. Ask them to offer free coupons to guests as compensation for any bad experiences.

- **Outsource for Cleaning**

Cleaning is one of the tasks which you will probably want to automate because it is not only time-consuming but also difficult if you really dislike cleaning the property yourself. Instead of taking on this chore, hire a pro from a good cleaning company to do the work for you.

If you give them consistent work, then these pros may reduce their hourly fee. Ensure that the cleaners are cleaning the property as you expect them to, and consider asking for a video call once the property has been turned over. You can also outsource this step to VAs to handle an inspection process.

Airbnb Property Management Companies

Not everyone has time to manage their Airbnb business all by themselves. Automation is important for most successful hosts in the hospitality industry. If you are someone who is not interested in managing the whole business by yourself and want to have everything managed by a third party, then property management companies are the safest option.

Airbnb property management is a lucrative industry, and you will still see profits but without worrying about all the management tasks that may start bogging you down once you get consistent bookings. All you have to do is lease the property and list it on Airbnb.

How Does Property Management Work?

Companies in the property management sector are usually firms that manage short-term and long-term rental businesses for a fee. Most of them charge based on how many guests you receive at your property.

They will handle one or all of the following tasks:

- Guest communication will be managed by the management company's trained professionals.
- All the check-in and check-out processes will be managed by them.
- A pro cleaner belonging to the company will visit the listing when a guest checks out.
- All the supplies that are considered essential for guests will be restocked by the company workers. Remember that after the restocking, hosts need to pay the bill to the management company depending on how much has been restocked.
- They will also help you manage your listing so that the number of clicks on your listing will increase.
- Some of these companies will participate in marketing on social media platforms so that your number of guest bookings will increase over time.

What are the Pros?

- **Saves Time and Energy**

When you make an agreement with a property management company, you need not worry about many tasks that used to take so much of your time. Everything will be managed by the company, and all you have to do is monitor how the process is being handled. If you are busy with a day job, then there is no other option more logical than this.

- **Easy to Handle Regulations and Research**

A good property management company will have its own legal team who are aware of the localities' regulations. They will provide you with better statistics related to the short-term rental industry and suggest properties for your future listings.

What are the Cons?

There are, however, some cons that hosts should be aware of before opting for this solution to manage their listings.

- **Higher Expenses**

Obviously, as someone will be managing all your listings and the necessary tasks that come with that job, you will be paying anywhere between 20 and 40 percent of what you earn from a booking to the property manager who is handling your listing. This is very costly for someone who is renting properties, and the profit margin will decrease drastically.

- **You Need to Sign a Contract**

When you let a management company take care of your listing, you will need to sign a contract for a period of time. As these companies expect a long-term, consistent relationship with their clients, it can be risky to sign a contract unless you are totally sure that they are the right company to go with.

Property Management Fee Structures

Property management companies will usually ask you to choose a fee structure when you sign a contract with them. You should be aware of different fee structures to ensure that your profit margins don't slip due to the fees you will be paying.

- **Commission Model**

When you choose this fee structure, you will be paying a certain percentage of your booking earnings to the company. The advantage of this model is that you will be paying a fee only when you get bookings for your listing. If there are more bookings, you will be paying more fees; on the other hand, if there are fewer bookings, you will be paying fewer fees. This is the default fee structure we suggest, especially if you are new to the Airbnb business.

- **Flat-Rate Model**

With time, when you have created a strong business with consistent bookings, you will be in a position to negotiate with a property management company to enter into a flat-fee contract, which is not dependent on the number of bookings. Based on their calculations, they will quote a one-time fee that you will need to pay in advance. The flat-rate model can save you a lot in fees during peak season, but during the low season, you may be paying more than you bring in.

It is a good idea to choose this fee structure only when you are confident that you will be generating enough income to offset the cost of management and saving money by avoiding commission fees.

Finding the Best Property Management Company

Airbnb property management has become a lucrative business, and so there is a lot of competition right now in that market. If you want to choose a management company, you need to be aware of the following checklist to be sure you're making a good decision.

- **Ratings and Referrals**

It is obvious that you need to check the ratings provided by other hosts about the company. Look at Google business and Yelp reviews to compare the feedback about different companies.

Don't just decide on a company after checking either 5-star or 1-star reviews. You need to check 3-star reviews as well to judge the company from a balanced point of view. By reading 3-star reviews, you will also get an idea of both the strengths and weaknesses of the company.

You might also find great companies by asking for referrals from other hosts in your locality.

- **Value for Money**

Ultimately, you need to choose a company that actually sees profits. It is not ideal for you to spend all of your earnings on a management company. Take an Excel spreadsheet, consider all the fees that are being charged, and calculate your Return on Investment (ROI) to decide on the best option.

- **Transparency**

Unfortunately, not all management companies are transparent. Check on sample reports or reviews to learn how each company is dealing with its reports. As you need to file taxes on your profits, it is important to work with a management company that charges only for work done.

- **Knowledge About the Local Market**

Even with a lot of features and working professionals, some management companies can be a bad fit for you, especially if they are unaware of your local market. Ensure that the company you are considering is aware of your surroundings and that they can suggest a pricing strategy. They also need to have enough knowledge to provide local recommendations for guests who stay at your listing.

Vacasa, Casago, Itrip, and Yonder are some of the popular property management companies that you may be interested in learning more about.

Scale Your Airbnb Business

To increase your profits, it is important to find ways to scale your business. Scaling doesn't just mean buying or leasing more properties to create new listings. Scaling also refers to improving how you manage your business, therefore fundamentally improving upon your quality of service and efficiency. There is always room to improve in the Airbnb industry, regardless of how profitable your listings are already. You need to scale your Airbnb business consistently to keep up with the market and earn money for the years ahead. Read on to learn how with tried and tested strategies.

Be Strategic with Your Cleaning Fees

Cleaning fees can be pretty high for listings, as it takes a lot of effort to get properties ready for the next guests after a stay. As it is also necessary to hire only the best professionals who can prepare the property as guests expect them to, most hosts have no other choice but to charge hefty cleaning fees.

A lot of guests, however, complain about high cleaning fees, as many of them claim that they take care of the property and do not feel the high fee is justified. While this may be true, hosts can't judge how well each guest is going to behave while on their property.

To scale your business properly, you may need to hire a short-term rental cleaning service that can do the work for all your listings at a discounted price. If you can strike a good deal for cleaning, then your guests can also receive a discount on their fees, resulting in more bookings and profits.

Rely on Property Management Software

Property management software helps hosts manage many different tasks for their listings. Most property management companies provide software that will let you easily manage and monitor your business activities. For example, you can keep a record of your inventory in different listings and manage them efficiently. The software will alert you with notifications when essentials need to be replaced or amenities need to be serviced.

With property management software, it becomes easier to calculate taxes, how much you have spent, and how much you need to stay profitable. When scaling your business, it is essential to have a handle on these details to be successful in the industry.

Look at the Data to Understand How to Scale

There is a constantly growing amount of data being provided by third-party companies regarding Airbnb properties to help you decide where to invest for your next listing. Services such as Airdna offer access to this data for a small fee. All you have to do is enter your locality and budget so that they can provide you with information regarding the type of property that guests are most interested in. All data that is provided is publicly available, and it takes Airbnb reviews, descriptions, and headings into account.

Compare Different Markets

When you are trying to scale your Airbnb business, you need to be aware of different markets that exist within the business itself. Here, market refers to the demographics that you are targeting, such as business travelers, tourists, and backpackers. For example, there are a lot of differences between providing service to business travelers versus tourists. The type of guests you are trying to attract will determine your budget and exposure. Your initial investment will also either increase or decrease depending on this factor.

Use services such as MarketMinder to get detailed analyses of different markets on Airbnb and decide what approach you need to take to scale your business. Diversify your business in different markets to scale in a way that will reflect in your profits, even if some markets experience losses.

Use Pricing Tools for Dynamic Pricing

When the number of listings you host increases, it may become more difficult to update and manage appropriate pricing for each property as time goes on. Especially during the low season, you may even need to change the price daily to ensure that you are not missing out on any bookings.

Instead of manually changing the prices for your nightly rates, you can use dynamic pricing tools that are available to hosts like you. Wiser, Wheelhouse, and Pricelabs are some of the options available that provide this service. These tools consider several factors such as keyword density, seasonality, and competitor bookings to keep your prices at the optimum point as parameters change over time.

Be Unique Among the Competition

It is important for successful Airbnb hosts to stay unique and offer the best in terms of amenities or hospitality service to ensure that they are winning more bookings than their competitors. When scaling your business, it is important to understand this and focus on building a brand that is unique to yourself.

If it will improve on the value of your listing, invest in high-end appliances or extend your property to include beautiful outdoor spaces for your guests. Pay attention to the details that will earn that "wow" factor, such as beautiful landscaping, comfortable furniture, or a clean fire pit with a stack of firewood ready to go. Scaling can be tough when you are trying to be unique in your locality. When you try to be unique with your listings and provide a five-star experience for your guests, your profit margins will increase.

Some ideas to try might include the following:

- Provide outstanding amenities that your competitors are not offering.
- Go above and beyond your competitors with great images and a professionally written description.
- Spend more on cleaning and ensure that you have all essentials stocked for every guest. Include items that will pleasantly surprise guests, such as new aromatherapy candles or complimentary facial scrub.

Chapter 8

Extras

This chapter is full of bonus information and tips for you to use as you build your Airbnb business.

How to Cope with the Slow Season

During the peak season, hosts will have guests booking their property even if it is mediocre because there is high demand. The slow season is when it is possible to separate great hosts from the not-so-great hosts. If you want to generate profits throughout the year from your properties, then you need to be aware of some of the techniques for getting bookings during the slower months.

Hosts who are new to the Airbnb business tend to have the misconception that their properties need to be rented at low prices during the dull season in order to earn profits. While this may be true for some properties and localities, it is not the only rule that you need to follow. Price adjustment is important, but it should not be the only strategy that you use.

Warning:

Remember that the following tactics can make your listing more flexible, but there is also risk involved whenever you make changes to established practices when it comes to running your business. So, before proceeding with these tactics, be sure you are making a good decision for your unique situation. Follow the precautions and safety measures mentioned in previous chapters.

- **Sign Up for "Airbnb Event Space"**

You can rent out your properties for daytime events. Peerspace and Splacer are two companies that can help you secure clients who host events depending on your property's size and the number of people it can accommodate. One good thing about this option is that all events will happen during daytime hours, lessening the chance that your neighbors will be disturbed.

Events will be anything from meetings to photo or film shoots, and sometimes might even be medium-size conferences. For this strategy to be viable, your property should be in a great urban location with lots of space.

- **Remove Extra Person Charges**

During the busier months, Airbnb hosts often charge extra person fees if there are more than the allowed number of guests on the property. An extra person fee is usually considered an aggressive pricing strategy, as it can greatly increase the profit potential for your business.

In slow seasons, however, it is recommended that you don't charge as much for these fees. For example, if the maximum number of guests allowed is four, then charge only if the number increases to five, and not so much that it would deter guests from booking with you. If you want to ensure that your properties are always booked during the dull season, then charge only half of the normal extra person fee.

- **Turn on Instant Book**

Many hosts feel uncomfortable with the instant book option provided on Airbnb. Typically, when you turn on the instant book option, guests will be able to book the property immediately without needing to send a request to the host. Instant bookings are great for guests, especially if they are planning last-minute trips.

During the slow season, we suggest you turn on this option. Turning on the instant book option will also increase your ranking in search results, making it easier to get more bookings. For hosts, it is also possible to cancel the booking if you find the guest sketchy and you are not willing to host them. Airbnb will not charge you a penalty for doing so, making this the leading tactic for your Airbnb business during the dull season.

- **Relax the House Rules**

House rules can be a turnoff for many guests and can lead to you losing out on a booking for your property. While strict house rules are important during the busy season, they can have a negative effect on your total number of bookings during the slower season, when you should be making your listing attractive to the widest possible audience.

It is highly recommended that you ease some of your house rules during this time. For example, if you don't usually allow dogs at your property, remove this rule and allow dogs for the season. You could also allow parties with reasonable conditions. Use devices such as NoiseAware to ensure that the guests are not making too much noise and disturbing neighbors. With a proprietary algorithm, NoiseAware measures not only how loud a space is but also how long it lasts.

How does NoiseAware work?

Purchase the NoiseAware device and install it on your property. Ensure that the device is out of reach of guests just to be safe. You can then link the device to your mobile phone via the NoiseAware app that is available on both the Google Play Store and Appstore. You can then switch it on so that the device can track noise in decibels and give you live tracking information on the app. Remember that NoiseAware will only track decibel information and not what your guests are talking about. Your guests' privacy will not be affected by this device.

- **Improve Your SEO**

Search engine optimization techniques are important for getting bookings, especially during the off-season. Make changes to your description and try to write catchy titles for your listing. Add words such as "discount" to your description or title to ensure that more potential guests see your listing when they search for properties.

Most of the guests that are traveling during the dull season are trying to find a deal, so providing them with discounts can be a great idea to attract more visitors.

- **Make Use of Referral Discounts**

Referral discounts can be a great tactic to get additional bookings from happy guests who have already stayed at your property. Once they check out from your property, use tools such as Hospitable to reach out to them about how their friends, family, or acquaintances can receive a 10-to-20% discount to stay at the property during the dull season. Don't forget to list the expiration date for the coupons to ensure that bookings can only be placed during the specified times.

To create your own discount coupons, head over to the "My Account" page on your Airbnb account and click on the "Create a Coupon" option. You can then send your coupon to guests with instructions to use them before a particular date.

- **Increase Discounts for Long Stays**

Hosts often provide discounts for when a guest books the property for a long period of time, such as a week or even up to two months. As longer stays provide consistent income, many hosts provide reasonable discounts even during the busy season. When a guest is looking for a long-term stay option, it is important to grab their attention by providing them with good discounts. You should, however, not go overboard and lose out on profits. Calculate your profits and approach with a pricing strategy that will ensure that your Airbnb business is both competitive and profitable during the slow season.

- **One-Night Bookings Should Be Allowed**

Most hosts do not usually allow guests who want to stay only for a night on the property. Many consider this risky because it can reduce the chances of getting the full week booked around those single nights. During slow months, however, these restrictions should be waived for better profits. It is important to improve your occupancy rates for the business to be profitable.

- **Provide a Flexible Cancellation Policy**

In a dull season, it should be your topmost priority to ease up on rules that are reducing your occupancy rates. One of the major rules that can turn off guests is a strict cancellation policy. Provide the instant cancellation option so that guests will be motivated to book your property.

- **Focus on Business Travelers**

Business travelers will always be traveling no matter if it is the summer or winter season, so your listings should be focused on these demographics when appropriate. Adjust your amenities so that business travelers will be more inclined to book your property. For example, a high-speed internet connection can be a tempting offer for business travelers, as they usually need to stay connected to the outside world. You could also invest in a fancy coffee machine if you are hosting business events or conferences.

- **Optimize Rates**

The most important tactic of all, however, will be to optimize your rates for each property. Use dynamic pricing tools to automatically reduce your rates when there is less demand or fewer searches.

You should be able to hold on until the peak season resumes by employing these techniques.

Common Mistakes to Avoid

Airbnb hosting can become complex and demanding quickly, especially if you don't have a strategy for making your property desirable to guests. We will take a look at some of the common mistakes that hosts make so you can avoid them yourself and earn good profits with the business in the long run.

1. Not Trying Out Airbnb as a Guest

It is a shocking fact, but a lot of hosts on Airbnb don't actually try different properties as guests themselves. Don't make this mistake because you are missing out on a lot of information and real-life experience regarding how other hosts are handling their business. Instead of spending hundreds of hours researching how to maximize profits with your Airbnb business, try visiting some of the popular properties in your area and checking out what other hosts are doing to wow their guests. Staying in a couple of properties can help you explore different strategies that are being used by successful hosts.

Learn about the following practices by staying as a guest yourself:

- ideas for welcoming guests
- how other hosts are managing the check-in and check-out process

- what amenities other hosts are providing
- how other hosts create manuals or guest guides
- how much space other hosts provide

Entrepreneurs in the hotel management business would not open a new hotel without ever having been in one of them already. Similarly, as a host, you need to experience being a guest yourself before starting a business with Airbnb.

2. Not Having a Proactive Pricing Strategy

For better profits, you should use a dynamic pricing strategy. Many Airbnb hosts are not keen to have a dynamic pricing strategy because they think that it will reduce their income over time. However, this is simply not true. All successful hosts use a proactive pricing strategy. A proactive pricing strategy involves anticipating both market and competitor changes and adjusting prices accordingly based on data-driven insights.

Conclusion

We hope our comprehensive guide will help you achieve your dreams in the Airbnb business. In addition to gaining theoretical knowledge about Airbnb, we hope you have also gained a better understanding of the practical principles and step-by-step instructions for making your short-term rental business successful.

Being a host in the Airbnb business requires patience and skill to overcome the hurdles that may arise during your journey. This book will help you understand all the skills that you need to develop to make your hosting business a long-term success. With the information learned from this book, we want you to make huge profits with your listings.

Remember that reading books is only the first step in starting your business. You need to be confident that you are capable of handling the nuances associated with running an Airbnb business. In my personal experiences, irrespective of how complicated, hard, and competitive the Airbnb business becomes, I've always loved doing it because I love pleasing guests who want to have a great experience during their stays.

By listing my properties, I believe that I am helping people rather than just running a business.

In an Airbnb business, the only way to make profit is to provide value to your guests. They are not worried about your profit margins or about your business scaling; all they care about is their experience at your property. When you start to provide a consistent and unforgettable experience to your guests, your profits will grow. When you care only about your business, it makes it hard for you to make profits. You need to value guests and their experience in order to reap the rewards of a successful Airbnb business.

With millions of people keen to start traveling again after easing pandemic restrictions around the world, we are currently seeing a new surge in the tourism and hospitality industry. This is the perfect time for you to take charge and become a part of the fast-growing Airbnb opportunities.

Before leaving us, take a look at some of the third-party tools in the following section that you can use to help your Airbnb business thrive.

Bonus: Tools for Your Airbnb Business

The Airbnb business has the potential to make you a millionaire if you can scale your business like many others who have already done so in the U.S. and all over the world. To help you manage and scale your Airbnb business, you need to be aware of several tools available from different developers and companies.

While there are some free tools, most of the tools that work well will charge you for the services they provide.

Dynamic Pricing Tools

- **Wheelhouse**

Wheelhouse is an online tool that helps you to easily customize prices depending on your expected profit margins.

Website Link: https://www.usewheelhouse.com

- **Rate Genie**

Rate Genie is a dynamic pricing tool that is focused on working with short-term rental services such as Airbnb. It is not just focused on Airbnb but extends its services to other hosting services as well.

Website Link: https://rategenie.io

- **Price Labs**

Price Labs is a tool that was developed to help property managers easily manage their listings. If you have more than one listing on Airbnb, then Price Labs is the best option because it uses a subscription model instead of a commission model.

Website Link: https://hello.pricelabs.co

Automated Messaging Tools

Most of the guest communications that will be required of you can be automated using the tools provided below.

- **Hospitable**

Hospitable is the most popular guest communication tool available on the market right now for hosts. It has a simple UI and hundreds of templates for you to use and quickly respond to a guest query.

Website Link: https://hospitable.com

- **Host Tools**

Host Tools is a set of tools that hosts can use to manage their Airbnb business. It is cheaper and also offers a lot of guest communication template options.

Website Link: https://hosttools.com

- **IGMS**

IGMS is an automated messaging tool that is used as an alternative to Smartbnb. While Smartbnb is of a high standard, it sometimes has integration issues that IGMS solves effectively.

Website Link: https://www.IGMS.com

Airbnb Channel Managers

If you are not just hosting using Airbnb but switching between several other channels, such as booking.com and Trip Adviser, then you can use the following tools.

- **Tokeet**

With Tokeet, it is easy to manage your listings from different channels using the same UI. You can maintain guest communication and change pricing either from the web or through the mobile app.

Website Link:https://www.tokeet.com

- **Guesty**

Guesty does all the same things that Tokeet does but also has a website builder for hosts to easily redirect from websites to their listing addresses.

Website Link: https://www.guesty.com

Tools to Create Digital Guide Books

Digital guidebooks help hosts to easily communicate with guests regarding instructions or rules that need to be followed during their stay. You can create beautiful digital guides with the help of the following tools.

- **Touch Stay**

Touch Stay helps hosts create welcome books for their listing. These guides are usually aesthetic and considered elegant.

Website Link: https://touchstay.com

- **Hostfully**

Hostfully is a digital guidebook creator. You can create a custom guide book for different guests depending on the season they are visiting with the help of this tool.

Website Link: https:/www.hostfully.com

Airbnb Market Research and Analysis Tool

When it comes to market research and analysis, either for your competition or your locality, there is no better tool than Airdna. Airdna provides analytical and statistical data of different types for you to make smart investment decisions.

Website Link: https://www.AirDNA.co

Airbnb Tool for SEO

Rank Breeze helps you to find popular keywords that guests are searching in your locality. Rank Breeze also offers a tool that automatically writes descriptions for your listings.

Website Link: https://rankbreeze.com

Other Important Tools and Websites Mentioned in this Book

- **Earnest**

A website that uploads research and findings about host demographics.

Website Link: https://www.earnest.com

- **Mashvisor**

A comparison tool that can be used to compare earnings and research reports.

Website Link: https://mashvisor.com

- **Meetup**

A networking tool where you can meet your fellow Airbnb hosts to share your strategies and work together.

Website Link: https://meetup.com

- **Upwork**

A freelancer website that hosts can use to hire virtual assistants for their Airbnb business.

Website Link: https://upwork.com

- **Mailchimp**

An email marketing tool that can be used to easily reach out to your previous or upcoming guests with just a click.

Website Link: https://mailchimp.com

- **Vacasa**

A popular rental management company used by Airbnb hosts.

Website Link: https://www.vacasa.com

- **Casago**

Another popular rental management company used by Airbnb hosts.

Website Link: https://casago.com

- **Itrip**

A property management company that focuses mostly on vacation rentals.

Website Link: https://www.itrip.net

- **Yonder**

A property management company that also focuses on vacation rentals.

Website Link: https://www.yondervacationrentals.com

Thank You

I want to give a big thank you to everyone who has bought my book. I hope you enjoyed the book and found it helpful.

If you could please take a moment to write a review on the platform, it would mean a lot to me. Your reviews help other people find my work and enjoy it too. It will also help me write the kind of books that will help you get the results you want in your Airbnb business.

Thanks again for taking the time to read my work and I hope to hear from you soon!

>> Leave a review on Amazon US <<
>> Leave a review on Amazon UK <<

References

A Step-by-Step Guide on How to List on Airbnb. (2018, November 26). Guesty. https://www.guesty.com/blog/step-by-step-guide-how-to-list-on-airbnb/

Airbnb amenities: the must-haves and the "wow" factor extras. (n.d.). Guestready. https://www.guestready.com/blog/airbnb-amenities-tips/

Airbnb Cancellation Policies | The Ultimate Guide. (n.d.). Hostaway. https://www.hostaway.com/airbnb-cancellation-policies/

Airbnb Cleaning Checklist. (2021, November 11). PriceLabs. https://hello.pricelabs.co/airbnb-cleaning-checklist/

Airbnb House Rules: Actionable Tips and Templates | Hospitable.com. (2020, September 7). Hospitable. https://hospitable.com/airbnb-house-rules/

Folger, J. (2021, January 24). *Airbnb: Advantages and Disadvantages.* Investopedia. https://www.investopedia.com/articles/personal-finance/032814/pros-and-cons-using-airbnb.asp

iGMS. (2019, November 27). *Airbnb rules: 6-Step checklist to stay within the law.* IGMS. https://www.igms.com/airbnb-rules/

Karani, A. (2019, August 7). *The 4 Steps of Airbnb Market Research. Investment Property Tips* | Mashvisor Real Estate Blog. https://www.mashvisor.com/blog/steps-airbnb-market-research/

McInnis, R. (2020, January 24). *AirBnB Taxes: Everything You Need to Know for 2020 Tax Season.* Picnic Tax. https://www.picnictax.com/airbnb-tax-guide/

Nix, D. (n.d.). *The Ultimate Insurance Guide for Airbnb® Hosts.* Www.steadily.com. https://www.steadily.com/blog/airbnb-insurance-guide